Minute Meditations for the Real World

Unlocking Peace and Productivity in Minutes a Day

VitalSpark Synergy

© **Copyright 2024 VitalSpark Synergy - All rights reserved.**

The content contained within this book may not be reproduced, duplicated or transmitted without direct written permission from the author or the publisher.

Under no circumstances will any blame or legal responsibility be held against the publisher, or author, for any damages, reparation, or monetary loss due to the information contained within this book, either directly or indirectly.

Legal Notice:

This book is copyright protected. It is only for personal use. You cannot amend, distribute, sell, use, quote or paraphrase any part, or the content within this book, without the consent of the author or publisher.

Disclaimer Notice:

Please note the information contained within this document is for educational and entertainment purposes only. All effort has been executed to present accurate, up to date, reliable, complete information. No warranties of any kind are declared or implied. Readers acknowledge that the author is not engaged in the rendering of legal, financial, medical or professional advice. The content within this book has been derived from various sources. Please consult a licensed professional before attempting any techniques outlined in this book.

By reading this document, the reader agrees that under no circumstances is the author responsible for any losses, direct or indirect, that are incurred as a result of the use of the information contained within this document, including, but not limited to, errors, omissions, or inaccuracies.

Table of Contents

TABLE OF CONTENTS 5

INTRODUCTION 1

PART I: MEDITATION ESSENTIALS FOR THE BUSY BEE 3

CHAPTER 1: MEDITATION UNVEILED 5
    MEDITATION MYTHS VS TRUTHS 5
    THE SIMPLICITY AND FLEXIBILITY OF MEDITATION 11

CHAPTER 2: BENEFITS OF MEDITATION FOR THE BUSY INDIVIDUAL 15
    IMMEDIATE BENEFITS 16
    LONG-TERM BENEFITS 18
    QUICK MEDITATION METHODS 26
        Breath Awareness 26
        Body Scan 28
        Listening Practice 29
        Mantra Recitation 32
        Portable Zen 33
        Walking Meditation 34
        The Attitude of Gratitude 34
        Movement-Based Practices 36

PART II: KICK-STARTING YOUR QUICK MEDITATION PRACTICE 39

CHAPTER 4: CRAFTING YOUR INSTANT ZEN ZONE 41
    THE IMPORTANCE OF SPACE 41
    TRANSFORM ANY LOCATION 45

CHAPTER 5: FAST-TRACK TECHNIQUES 51
    POSTURE, SETTING, AND FOCUS 52
    FAST-TRACK MICRO-MEDITATION METHODS 53

CHAPTER 6: OVERCOMING TIME-RELATED OBSTACLES 57
    THE HUSTLE AND BUSTLE 57
    STRATEGIES FOR INTEGRATING MEDITATION 61

PART III: GOAL-ORIENTED MEDITATION FOR THE BUSY MIND 67

CHAPTER 7: QUICK STRESS AND ANXIETY RELIEF 69

THE NEW NORMAL? 69
- Why Overloaded Schedules Demand Stress Relief Mastery 71

BEATING STRESS AND ANXIETY IN THE MOMENT 73
- Progressive Muscle Relaxation (PMR) 73
- Grounding Exercises 74
- Bilateral Stimulation 74
- Vocal Toning 75
- Mental Imagery 75
- Finger Counting Breaths 76
- Quick Coherence Technique 77
- Dancing Meditation 77

CHAPTER 8: QUICK BOOSTS FOR HEALTH AND WELLNESS 81

REDEFINING HEALTH AND RECOVERY 82
- The Interconnected Pillars of Peak Human Thriving 83
- The Regenerative Power of Brief Mindfulness 86

PRIORITIZING QUALITY WELL-BEING 88
- Busy Person's Guide to Optimizing Sleep Quality 90

CHAPTER 9: BOOSTING WORK EFFICIENCY AND CREATIVITY 95

UNMASKING WORKPLACE BURNOUT 96
- The Unrelenting Pace: When Productivity Becomes a Pitfall 96
- The Autonomy Deficit: Micromanagement's Insidious Impact 97
- The Stagnation Trap: When Growth Stalls, Motivation Wanes 98
- The Culture of Overwork: Blurring the Line Between Job and Identity 99
- The Toxicity Factor: Unhealthy Workplace Dynamics 99
- The Societal Pressures: Navigating Unrealistic Expectations 100
- The Psychological Toll: When Burnout Becomes a Vicious Cycle 101

MINDFULNESS HACKS FOR THE WORKPLACE TO BOOST PRODUCTIVITY AND INNOVATION 102
- Body Scan for Creativity 102
- Breath Awareness for Focus 103
- Mindful Listening for Effective Communication 103
- Nature Breaks for Stress Relief 104
- Mindfulness in Meetings 104
- Practical Workplace Meditation Tips 105
- What to Avoid 106

CHAPTER 10: CULTIVATING PERSONAL GROWTH IN LIMITED TIME 108

THE UNTAPPED CATALYSTS: SELF-AWARENESS AND EMPATHY 109
AWAKENING THROUGH THE MOMENTS: EMBEDDING MINDFULNESS 111

    At Your Desk or Work Station 112
    While Commuting or Running Errands 112
    In Meetings or Group Settings 113
    In Moments of Downtime or Transition 114
  The Benefits Compound Over Time 115

PART IV: INTEGRATING MINDFULNESS INTO YOUR DAILY ROUTINES 118

CHAPTER 11: MAKING MEDITATION A SEAMLESS PART OF LIFE 120

  Sense and Sensibility: Multitasking 121
    Why Mindfulness + Routine Tasks = Productivity Boost 122
  Navigating the Currents of Modern Life: Quick Techniques for Presence, Stress Reduction, and Seamless Meditation 125
    Mindful Sustenance: Eating With Presence 125
    The Sacred Stroll: Walking With Intention 126
    The Sound of Stillness: Listening With Mindful Presence 127
    Seamless Integration: Establishing Consistent Meditation Habits 128
    Techniques for Seamless Meditation Integration 129

CHAPTER 12: IMPROVING MEDITATION WITH TECHNOLOGY 132

  Merging of Ancient and New Age 133
    How Tech Tools Can Enhance the Journey 136
    How Tech Can Enable Distraction 137
  Blending Tradition With Innovation 139
    Meditating Through the Digital Lens 139
    Integrating Technology and Tradition 141
    App Suggestions 143

CHAPTER 13: SCIENTIFICALLY SOUND PRACTICES 148

  The Science of Everyday Meditation 149
    Psychological Benefits 150
    Cognitive Benefits 150
    Physical Benefits 151
    Practical Applications for Busy Lives 152
    Techniques for Quick Meditation Sessions 153
    Long-Term Benefits of Regular Quick Meditation 154
  Say What? 156

CONCLUSION 158

REFERENCES 161

SPECIAL BONUS!

Want this Bonus book for Free?

Introduction

We can't always change what's happening around us, but we can change what happens within us. –Andy Puddicombe

When someone first mentioned "meditation," I pictured a contortionist trying to get into a lotus pose all tied up like a pretzel or maybe one of those yoga influencers casually floating into a dancer pose while situating triplets into the minivan. But, of course, true meditation doesn't require that level of multitasking mastery.

Finding time to breathe, let alone meditate, can seem impossible in the hustle and bustle of our modern lives. For many, the idea of sitting in silence for hours feels incompatible with the demands of a fast-paced lifestyle. But what if I told you that unlocking peace, productivity, and well-being doesn't require hours of your day or becoming human origami? Imagine transforming your hectic schedule with just a few minutes of mindful practice each day, tapping into a limitless vault of zen through bite-sized mindful mini-escapes. Welcome to *Minute Meditations for the Real World*, a revolutionary approach to mindfulness tailored for those with minimal time and maximum responsibilities.

Traditional meditation practices can feel out of reach in today's rapid-fire world, where every second counts and stress is constant. This book is here to bridge that gap. By stripping away the myths and misconceptions, *Minute Meditations for the Real World* presents meditation in a way that is accessible, practical, and profoundly effective for the busiest individuals.

What makes this read a transcendental game-changer is its laser focus on short, impactful practices that can be seamlessly integrated into your daily routine. Whether you're navigating the chaos of a demanding job, managing a household, or juggling multiple commitments, this book offers you the tools to find moments of tranquility and clarity amid the madness.

Throughout our journey, we will explore the indispensable role of meditation in thriving amidst today's relentless pace. You'll gain insights into the evolution of meditation, understand its enduring relevance, and discover how it can be adapted to fit even the tightest schedules. This road map is designed for those who believe they don't have a minute to spare, showing you that you do—right there within your busy life.

Imagine navigating your day with the calm clarity of a mindfulness maverick, effortlessly transitioning from the boardroom to the living room, from conference calls to family dinners, all while maintaining an unshakable inner equilibrium. This is the promise of *Minute Meditations for the Real World*—integrating ancient wisdom with modern practicality to help you achieve lasting peace, health, productivity, and efficiency.

Part I:
Meditation Essentials for the Busy Bee

Chapter 1:

Meditation Unveiled

If you want to conquer the anxiety of life, live in the moment, live in the breath. –
Amit Ray

Too many people picture this practice as some ultra-serious, monastery-approved ritual requiring hours of torturous stillness. Or, they think you need an invisibility cloak to sneak away from life's insanity before you can even attempt it. Well, prepare to have those antiquated notions blown straight out of your third eye!

Stripping meditation down to its essence, you'll see it's more about expanding awareness than escaping reality—more about embracing simplicity than grueling over complexity. We're going to blow the doors wide open and make mindfulness mastery infinitely more accessible for any of us mere mortal multitaskers.

I'll break it down in a snackable, no-nonsense way, demystifying all the cryptic myths while keeping things candidly real. You'll be pleasantly surprised at how uncomplicated and infinitely flexible this ancient practice can be when distilled to its fundamentals.

Meditation Myths vs Truths

Let's unpack some of the biggest meditation myths and misconceptions out there.

False information have been pollinating minds for way too long, leaving people too intimidated to even attempt this ancient awesomeness.

- **Myth 1: Meditation requires hours of practice every day to see any benefits.**

    o **Reality:** While regular practice is beneficial, even short meditation sessions can yield noticeable improvements in mental clarity, emotional balance, and overall well-being. Consistency matters more than duration in meditation practice.

- **Myth 2: Meditation is all about clearing your mind of every single thought.**

    o **Reality:** The idea of having to purge your brain of any stray thoughts is about as realistic as trying to lasso a hummingbird. Our minds are thought-generating machines, which is perfectly normal. Meditation isn't about forcefully silencing the chatter but about noticing the chatter without frantically trying to change the channel. Meditation is about awareness. It's an exercise in conscious, non-judgmental awareness, making room for thoughts to simply arise and pass without getting violently ushered to the recesses of the mind.

- **Myth 3: It's just an unproductive waste of time.**

    o **Reality:** I can't blame the skeptics for this one—the idea of slowing down and just breathing for extended periods can feel criminally unambitious in our supercharged culture. But meditation is strength training for your attention muscle. By training your mental focus, you're enhancing your ability to channel concentration exactly where you want it. Expect a significant decline in irresistible urges to impulse-check your Instagram every 2.5 seconds or stress-spiral about some trivial mishap. Your mind masters the art of quickly recovering its center and directing its energy productively. It's pure focused productivity.

- **Myth 4: It's just pseudoscience with no real benefits.**
    - **Reality:** Despite meditation's longstanding roots, the clinical research around its impacts is surprisingly robust. We're talking about reams of peer-reviewed studies from major universities and medical institutions linking the practice to all sorts of evidence-based upsides. From reducing stress and anxiety to improving focus, emotional regulation, well-being, and even physical markers like blood pressure, the data is undeniable (12 Science-Based Benefits of Meditation. 2022). Neuroscientists have even directly observed changes in brain activity and gray matter density in long-term meditators (Hölzel et al. 2011). So, while some folks may still dismiss it as pseudoscientific snake oil, the rapidly growing body of empirical research says otherwise. This peace-promoting party trick is the real deal!

- **Myth 5: You need to attend years of intensive training to get it right.**
    - **Reality:** While there's certainly no cap on how deep the mindfulness journey can take you, the entry point is far more accessible than people realize. You could enroll in a monastical program or splurge on a dozen intensive retreats to acquire advanced techniques. But you can also pick up the basic methods via an intro class, app, book, or online video, possibly even this one you're

reading right now! From there, it's simply about consistency to experience the fruits.

- **Myth 6: It's religious... or anti-religious?**
  - **Reality:** Mention meditation and some people can get pretty worked up. But this practice simply isn't tied to any specific theology or dogma. It doesn't require converting your belief system whatsoever. You can integrate a meditation habit seamlessly, whether you're an atheist, agnostic, Jehovah's Witness, or Jedi. Some find it enhances their spiritual leanings, while others use it solely for focus or stress relief. The choice of how to frame it is yours.

- **Myth 7: You need to twist yourself into a pretzel pose to do it properly.**
  - **Reality:** While elaborate yogi flexibility definitely isn't required, I can't blame folks for thinking meditation is an extreme circus act. We've all seen those stock photos of the serene Buddhist monk casually levitating in full lotus pose, looking more unruffled than a glazed donut. That's the way they market it to us. But the truth is, you can meditate just as effectively in any position that keeps your spine relatively straight and shoulders relaxed. Whether that's seated on a cushion, plopped in an office chair, lying down, or even standing up. No elaborate yogi flexibility is necessary. The only feat you're aiming for is mental presence.

- **Myth 8: Meditation is only for certain personality types.**
  - **Reality:** Meditation is accessible to people of all personalities, backgrounds, and ages. Meditation can be

adapted to suit your needs and preferences, whether you're naturally calm or easily distracted.

- **Myth 9: It's way too new age.**
    - **Reality:** I get it; some terms around meditation can seemingly venture into a serious "mystical botanical vortex." Terms like awakening higher consciousness and aligning your chakras can trigger eye-rolls quicker than a bad toupee. But, beneath all that esoteric language lies a refreshingly practical toolkit for cultivating a calmer, more aware mindset. You can keep it grounded or go full tilt with the terminology. It's a choose-your-own-adventure scenario.

- **Myth 10: It's just navel-gazing and self-indulgent.**
    - **Reality:** Meditation isn't about solipsistic navel-gazing. In fact, it expands your perspective to dissolve that hyper-individualistic narrative and realize your interconnection with all beings. You become less self-obsessed and more attuned to the shared human experience. You become less judgy and more empathetic. You become less reactive and more responsive. It's a potent paradox; by going inward, you inevitably transcend those exclusively self-centered blinders.

- **Myth 11: You need a quiet environment to meditate.**
    - **Reality:** While a quiet space can be helpful, meditation can be practiced in various environments, including busy places or even during daily activities. The key is to cultivate inner focus and mindfulness regardless of external distractions.

- **Myth 12: Meditation is only for reducing stress.**
    - **Reality:** While stress reduction is a significant benefit of meditation, it offers a wide range of advantages beyond that. These include improved focus, enhanced creativity, better emotional regulation, and increased self-awareness.
- **Myth 13: You need to spend tons of money on classes and gear.**
    - **Reality:** The meditation-industrial complex would certainly love you to think lavish expenditures are required: designer cushions, fashionable accessories, infinite app subscriptions, and retreat center memberships. But here's the beautifully democratic truth: the most potent elements of the practice are completely free and accessible to anyone, anywhere. All you need is your breath, your body, and a semblance of patience. Certainly, there are enriching programs and gear that can enhance the experience if that's your jam. But the core skill of witnessing the present moment in a relaxed, lucid way is available at no charge.
- **Myth 14: Meditation is a quick fix for all problems.**
    - **Reality:** Meditation can be transformative, but it's not a magic solution that instantly solves all issues. It's a practice that requires consistency and patience to see long-term benefits. It's a tool for personal growth rather than a quick fix.

- **Myth 15: It's something you eventually master and complete.**
  - **Reality:** Our addicted-to-achievement minds desperately want meditation to be another item to checkmark or frame for our wall of achievements. The practice is inherently never fully "complete." It's an ever-evolving journey of awakening to the pricelessness and richness of each passing, impermanent moment. You simply continue deepening your familiarity with presence, with periods of losing that wakefulness and having to begin again... and again... and again. Rather than a final destination, it's an infinitely forking path with vistas to experience at every bend. Judging your practice or obsessing over "success" completely misses the point. The only mastery is showing up, letting go, immersing in what's arising now, and then repeating that open awareness tomorrow.

There you have it: the big mythical beasts reframed through an imminently more grounded, rational lens. With the right context and dose of playful perspective, this ancient practice becomes pragmatic and relatively fuss-free for even the most frenzied multitaskers.

The Simplicity and Flexibility of Meditation

Let's address the mighty white elephant in the room upfront: the idea that meditating has to be this whole elaborate, picky production number. No way, José!

The beauty of meditation is its core simplicity. Sure, if you want to lean into the ornate ceremonial aspects, by all means, immerse in your Tibetan singing bowls and chakra chimes. They're great! But you can just as easily tap into the power of presence while lounging in pajama slacks on your living room floor. In its most basic form, meditation is the act of plopping your tush down and focusing your attention in a particular way for a stretch of time. That's the whole co-op right there. No dogma, special outfits, or cosmic initiations are required.

You're already doing this core meditational move multiple times per day without even realizing it. When you zone out during your morning shower, suddenly entranced by the water droplets cascading down the glass doors, or get mesmerized by the flames dancing in your backyard fire pit, or even when you get hopelessly absorbed in people-watching in a busy public space, those are all micro-meditations. The difference between a more formalized practice is the intentionality behind it. That's what gives the wandering mind traction and focus. Whether your anchor is your breath, a philosophical question, or visualizing an image in your mind's eye, you're simply reorienting where you consciously rest your awareness for a bit.

And here's the wildly liberating part: There is no one "right" way to do it. Meditating from the get-go is an exercise in finding what anchors and methods best resonate with your unique temperament and life rhythms as an individual, not what mainstream images of yogis on advice from self-help gurus might suggest. It could be lying flat on your back in bed simply noticing the rise and fall of your belly for five conscious breaths before getting up, or stealing away to a quiet corner and counting inhales and exhales during your lunch break. You could recite uplifting mantras silently while walking the aisles of a corner store. The possibilities are endless for infusing moments of centered presence into even the most mundane tasks.

Part of the fun is getting irreverent and bespoke with it. If a "traditional" seated cross-legged position feels like cruel torment, kick back in a recliner instead. Instead of a quiet room, maybe the background hum of a coffee shop helps your focus. The point is that at the end of the day, this is your unique journey into the present moment. Any prescriptions or dogmas are self-imposed limits that simply don't apply to everyone. Gone are the days of believing you need special circumstances, times, outfits, or props to be a "successful" meditator. It's all about seamlessly integrating pockets of purpose-driven attention into your already hectic routine. Meditation's true beauty and pragmatism lie in its portability and adaptability to whatever modern chaos fills your days. You can genuinely reap all the vitalizing benefits—reduced stress and anxiety, boosted focus and creativity, resilience against burnout—through cleverly positioning bite-sized practices whenever you've got a spare 60 seconds. All without needing to flee your life completely or adhere to a rigid, monastical schedule.

Those quick pauses for conscious breathing while waiting at stoplights? Meditation. Silently reciting an uplifting mantra while changing that mountain of laundry over? You're meditating, baby. Even the act of setting a timer to purposefully bring your awareness back to this very moment counts as formal practice. It's simply about reorienting to the present space through whatever quirky method works for you at that moment. Once you start recognizing all the windows of opportunity for mini-meditations scattered throughout your day, it opens up a whole new lens on your messy, marvelous human existence. Turns out, every hiccup, delay, or waiting period is actually an invitation to press pause, take a conscious breath, and recenter yourself. After all, life's what you make of it, right?

Rather than steam shooting from your ears during your latest work Zoom call getting bombarded by circle-back synergy questions, you'll recognize it as an opportunity to silently bring your attention to the soles of your feet on the floor. When your kids inevitably launch into the latest heated battle over who got more appropriate milk proportions, you can briefly tune into the present play of sounds and body sensations. Shoot, getting stuck at a criminally long red light could become a pint-sized respite to bask in the simplicity of inhales and exhales.

This is the glory of a meditation practice tailored specifically for your unique and hectic life. It's not about transcending reality itself but consciously anchoring your presence to ride its ebbs and flows with more grace. It's about slowing down, even for a few conscious inhalations, so the frantic daily torrent doesn't carry you completely away from yourself.

By stripping the pretense and revelry, you reframe meditation as something delightfully straightforward and infinitely integrable into whatever your day holds. So, forget what you think you knew about this ancient art of awareness. Modern meditation mastery is all about creatively infusing pockets of lucid presence into the course of your daily life. It's a sanity bookmark—your portal to more vitality.

The shift is more straightforward and infinitely more organic than you've been led to believe.

You made it through the demystification gauntlet! Meditation's truly accessible nature has been unveiled. Now, let's dip some toes into the waters of how much a little intentional presence can utterly uplevel your whole existence.

Chapter 2:

Benefits of Meditation for the Busy Individual

He who lives in harmony with himself lives in harmony with the universe. –Marcus Aurelius

I can hear the skeptics piping up louder than a foghorn: "Sure, sure, but what's actually in it for me besides some vaguely chill vibes?"

Well, prepare for your curious minds to be utterly blown. This chapter is an electrifying exposé on how a consistent meditation habit charged with a pragmatic presence can upgrade your overall operating system in ways you've only dreamed of. It's a whole-human-being level glow-up, covering both the inner landscape of well-being and peak productivity. It's entirely holistic. From learning to command your focus to slipping into creative flow states with casual ease, the cognitive and emotional upsides alone will have you jumping for joy. Add in resiliency potent enough to wrestle chronic burnout into submission, and you've got one compelling recipe for thriving.

We're not even scratching the surface of all the meta-benefits lying in wait. It dismantles the knee-jerk ego reactivity that probably sparks at least 73% of your interpersonal conflicts. Increased self-awareness, emotional mastery, and even scientifically validated boosts to physical health and longevity; it's all fair game.

The point is that meditation isn't just some relaxation trick. It's a transformative practice that can upgrade your entire operating system from root to stem if you're willing to commit to the journey.

Immediate Benefits

When most of us first encounter meditation, we probably think it's like a cosmic security blanket to anxiety binge on when the stresses of life feel a bit too extra.

For all the busy bees out there, permanently walking that razor's edge between feeling accomplished and feeling like you're on the world's hamster wheel, meditation is actually one of the most impactful productivity and stress-management tools. While certain aspects of mindfulness mastery do require patient cultivation over time, the core mechanic of bringing your awareness into the visceral here-and-now delivers tangible boosts to focus, emotional regulation, and resilience against burnout, practically from day one. It's like gradually building up a whole new muscle group for your mind.

Let's address that chronic kryptonite: daily stressors, a potent mix of overwhelm from infinite open tabs, looming deadlines, endless chores and to-dos, and a torrent of standard meetings. Even after just a few mindful minutes of conscious breathing or paying attention to your body, you help your brain and body return to a more balanced state. This grants you the perfect space to prioritize and tackle your growing to-do list with the grace of a zen master instead of feeling overwhelmed and constantly reacting to urgent tasks—a centered presence of being responsive instead of reactive.

From this vantage point, you're far likelier to handle obligations with poise. No more dopamine-chasing social media binges while you are deep in that big proposal or endlessly ruminating on what got said—or didn't—in some innocuous morning standup.

By persistently refreshing your mindful awareness throughout the day, you're batting away distracting thought loops before they can derail you too far off your mission-critical tracks. The clear-minded focus becomes your new default rather than constant tugs toward the nearest shiny distraction. Meditation equips you with enhanced abilities to slip into those coveted "flow" states. Those immersive pockets where distracting chatter dissolves, and you're fully absorbed in the energizing rhythm of the task at hand. It gives you instant access to clear and focused mental states by training your brain to relax unnecessary networks while boosting important task-related pathways. It's like you're piloting your consciousness with marksman-like precision rather than being battered about by random thoughts.

But what about when those stressful flare-ups inevitably kick your nervous system into false alarm mode, triggering the whole fight-or-flight menu of reactions? Well, that's where meditation's ability to cultivate resilience and self-regulation really shines.

Rather than compounding the panic by proliferating worst-case scenarios, your mindfulness enables you to drop anchor into the present moment; you observe your bodily sensations, racing thoughts, and emotional outbursts with a neutral distance instead of reacting with aversion. By not fighting against the turmoil or rushing to solve it, you create a space for the agitation to calm naturally. This allows for clearer thinking and better decision-making—perhaps the emails can wait until after lunch, or the deadline can be adjusted, or you might just need a quiet evening for self-care. These are the sorts of skillful, well-calibrated choices that mindful presence empowers. With each round of practiced mindfulness, this skill strengthens. Soon enough, you're no longer that jittery chihuahua routinely sent into panic by everyday stressors. You're cultivating an inner oak—steadfast, sturdy, and resilient even when gale-force winds kick up. This resilience pays exponential dividends in combating the prevalent pandemic of our time: burnout, a persistent threat that can affect even the most accomplished individuals. You're familiar with the symptoms—deep exhaustion, detachment, and the existential questioning of "Why am I even doing this?"

A diligent meditation practice is like an energizing underground river that constantly replenishes and reoxygenates your drive, clarity, and sense of bigger-picture purpose. All the shiny-object distractions, resentments, and psychological scar tissue get diligently filtered out. Frequent dips into the nourishing stream of presence help restore your vigor, curiosity, and knowledge of why you opted into this whole lifestyle or career in the first place. Priorities recalibrate, idealistic intention reforms, and you're back basking in the playfulness of flow.

Whether you're aiming to boost productivity or ward off burnout, daily meditation acts as a rejuvenating elixir for well-being. It loosens your fixations, soothes your nervous system, and reconnects you to reserves of energy and enthusiasm. Let's summarize the immediate benefits you can tap into:

- productivity enhancement
- emotional regulation
- immediate stress relief
- resilience against burnout
- rejuvenating well-being
- enhanced efficiency

And these immediate boosts are merely the appetizer to the full existential meal.

But for now, you're beginning to recognize why mindfulness belongs in any forward-thinking individual's tool kit. It's like a powerful upgrade for the human operating system, enhancing efficiency, stability, and overall processing capabilities.

Long-Term Benefits

Meditation has plenty of short-term perks that'll make your personal and professional juggling acts feel infinitely more sustainable—cupfuls of clarity, focus, and resilient calm amidst the chaos.

Beyond the mindful productivity hacks and stress-busting skills, this ancient art contains recipes for activating untapped dimensions of your innate human potential:; self-mastery, creativity, emotional intelligence, and an overall life upgrade. The deeper you immerse yourself in present-moment awareness over time, the more you'll start experiencing revelations. Accesses to whole new ways of being that most of us can barely conceive of in our dissociated rat-race norms.

For one, consistent meditation greases those existential gears toward an amplified sense of self-awareness and purpose alignment. In the beginning, the mindful lens simply highlights all the micro-behaviors, knee-jerk reactions, and outdated conditioning patterns that have been unconsciously driving your life's ride straight into ditches. But stick with consistent bursts of meditation, and steadily, you'll start peeling away those rusty layers of delusion, opening yourself up to the core of your authenticity. Rather than bobbing along on society's conveyor belt of expectations, you reunite with your true callings and deepest value systems as an individual. Priorities snap into focus, relationships transform, and you start showing up in this world with a profound sense of harmony. No longer confined by other people's narratives or lofty ideals about how you "should" behave or "should" be, you embody radical self-acceptance and navigate by your hard-won truths.

Speaking of transformation, meditation is a renovation for your emotional literacy, interpersonal communication skills, and overall leadership presence. Where you were once thrashing about in personal blind spots or petty egoic entanglements, suddenly it's like you have X-ray vision into your emotional depths. With time, the practice makes you more aware of your feelings, reactions, and interactions with others. It's an incredible presence; you're able to understand root motivations, see through superficial dramas, and respond to everything from micro-aggressions to mega-conflicts with deep compassion and understanding. Not only does this make you thrive from the boardroom to the living room, but it also enables you to transform interpersonal tensions when others are struggling. You become that eye of the storm that reorients people to their integrity.

Meditation leads to an awakening to something beyond productivity or profit—a deep connection to the beauty of existence, guiding you to a higher level of prosperity.

Instead of chasing hollow accomplishments or perpetually sacrificing your values on the altars of busyness, you begin approaching each moment with exceptional awareness and deep respect. The entire universe and your role in it solidifies into a beautiful cosmic choreography to embrace rather than resist. From this expanded perspective, you naturally enter into creative flow states. Hidden barriers in your mind fade away, unveiling endless wellsprings of inspiration, openness, and childlike wonder. You shed those ingrained identities as "not being a creative person," creating innovative solutions, envisioning new approaches, and even discovering entirely new creative paths fueled by passion. Life becomes a collaboration, with each interaction and decision unfolding from a place of presence. Let's summarize the profound impact of your dedication to meditation:

- amplified self-awareness
- purpose Alignment
- transformation of priorities and relationships
- enhanced emotional literacy, interpersonal communication, and leadership presence
- improved conflict resolution
- a more profound sense of connection and prosperity
- enhanced creative flow states and inspiration
- improved sense of identity
- improved innovation
- improved decision-making

While the immediate benefits of focus, balance, and calm are great, continue tuning into meditation's deeper impacts. It will optimize you far beyond any crude "productivity hacking" metrics. What starts as a simple practice to find balance expands into unlocking limitless human potential in all aspects: psychological, interpersonal, spiritual, and creative. It reconnects you to the pricelessness of the direct human experience itself.

Ultimately, meditation leads to a profound transformation into the purposeful person you were meant to be—a masterfully aware individual co-creating a beautiful life.

Enough with all the teasers about meditation's expansive capabilities. By now, your intrigue should be fully piqued about how integrating some mindful moments into your frantic schedule could be a complete game-changer.

SPECIAL BONUS!

Want this Bonus book for Free?

Chapter 3:

Choosing the Right Meditation Technique for You

> *It's a funny thing about life: Once you begin to take note of the things you are grateful for, you begin to lose sight of the things that you lack.* –Germany Kent

The thought of attempting to tame your mental Wild West through extended silent sitting sessions is probably feeling a bit ambitious. Your day-to-day hustle barely allows enough bandwidth to process social media reels, let alone spend whole hours on inner exploration.

This chapter is a freewheeling tour through all the delightfully bite-sized mindfulness styles crafted specifically for us hyper-scheduled pace-chasers of the modern era. We'll look into meditation's grab-n-go hits that seamlessly slide into even the most demanding calendar. These are potent micro-practices you can realistically incorporate into your day to take breaks and improve how you handle life's busy moments—a consistent micro-dosing of reoriented awareness to keep you smoothly cruising through the chaos. For us real-life multitaskers, the name of the game is quick-strike mindfulness, which requires minimal fuss but maximal self-attunement—techniques gentle enough to pull off at your desk mid-meeting haze yet potent enough to reorient your entire nervous system in a few stilled breaths. These are methods to zap you back into a state of primed readiness and focus, instantly offsetting those frantic mind spirals before they deplete you—meditations to slot in while commuting, exercising, prepping meals, heck, maybe even during commercial breaks.

Forget the typical images of challenging yoga poses. The techniques we'll explore transform any and every scenario into an opportunity to reclaim your clarity and calm through purposeful presence. The real secret to integrating meditation into your busy life is consistency, not grand gestures of renunciation. It's better to establish a simple daily routine of refreshing mindfulness than to chase an unrealistic ideal that never comes to fruition.

Quick Meditation Methods

Luckily for all of us mere mortals who are juggling numerous responsibilities in continuous rotation, the wisdom of this ancient practice has transformed into very easy-to-use methods.

There are micro-methods for micro-moments, like espresso shots of clarity that we can realistically slurp with gusto throughout our days. You'll never look at stoplights, waiting rooms, or inbox lulls the same way again; you'll recognize them as organic mindfulness opportunities, quick redirectors for recalibrating your frazzled nervous systems back towards equilibrium.

So, without further ado, let's look at some of meditation's finest grab-n-go delicacies for you to sample:

Breath Awareness

Perhaps the most classic and accessible of all mindful methods, breath awareness is as simple as reverently tuning into the subtle flow of air nuzzling its way into your nostrils and belly with each inhalation and exhalation.

You're not trying to control or regulate the breath, just gently riding its naturally soothing rhythm as an entry point back into presence. Beginners can keep it simple and just count cycles from 1 to 10. More advanced practitioners might explore nuances like the pauses between inhales and exhales or even visualize the breath's internal pathways. The true magic, though, is that even just 5 to 10 conscious breaths act like an ice bath for simmering tensions, creating a refreshed space for receptivity and discernment. Additionally, you can mix things up by engaging in specific breathing practices such as diaphragmatic breathing, alternate nostril breathing, or the 4-7-8 technique. These practices can be done in only 5 minutes and have been shown to significantly reduce stress levels, offering a quick and effective way to bring calmness and clarity to your day.

Diaphragmatic Breathing

1. Sit or lie down and relax your body, placing one hand on your chest and the other on your abdomen.

2. Slowly and deeply inhale through your nose, feeling your abdomen rise as you fill your lungs with air. Keep your chest relatively still while focusing on expanding your diaphragm.

3. Exhale slowly through your mouth, feeling your abdomen deflate as you release the air from your lungs. Try to fully empty your lungs before the next inhale, contracting your abdominal muscles.

4. Continue this breathing pattern for a few minutes, focusing on the sensation of your breath filling and leaving your body.

Alternate Nostril Breathing

1. Sit comfortably with your spine straight. Place your left hand on your left knee with your palm facing upward.

2. Use your right thumb to close your right nostril and inhale deeply through your left nostril.

3. Then, use your right ring finger to close your left nostril while releasing your right nostril. Exhale completely through your right nostril.

4. Now, inhale deeply through the right nostril while still keeping the left nostril closed.

5. Switch sides and exhale through the left nostril.

6. Repeat this cycle for a couple of minutes, alternating nostrils with each breath.

4-7-8 Breathing Technique

1. Sit or lie down comfortably, placing the tip of your tongue against the roof of your mouth behind your front teeth, keeping your lips slightly parted.

2. Inhale quietly through your nose for a count of 4 seconds, filling your lungs with air.

3. Hold your breath for a count of 7 seconds, keeping the air in your lungs.

4. Slowly and audibly exhale through your mouth for a count of 8 seconds, emptying your lungs of air.

5. Repeat this breathing pattern for a few cycles, maintaining a calm and steady rhythm.

Body Scan

If wandering attention is your personal kryptonite, a systematic body scan may bring you back to your physical presence like nothing else.

This involves slowly sweeping your awareness from toes to crown, or reverse, taking a clear inventory of any clenching, tingling, pulsating, or softening happening in each body region. You're not trying to fix, judge, or resist the somatic experience; just bear witness to all the sensations through your body in the very moment.

While guided body scans can last 20 minutes or more, by quickly laser-combing all quadrants in lightning-fast succession, as little as 60 seconds will also do the trick.

1. Sit or lie down and close your eyes.

2. Take a few deep breaths, inhaling slowly through your nose and exhaling through your mouth, allowing your breath to deepen and relax your body naturally.

3. Shift your attention to your body, starting with your feet. Notice any sensations, tension, or areas of comfort.

4. As you inhale, imagine sending relaxation and warmth to your feet.

5. Gradually move your awareness upward to your ankles, calves, knees, and thighs, consciously relaxing and releasing any tension you may be holding in these areas with each breath.

6. Bring your attention to your pelvic area, lower back, and abdomen. Feel the gentle rise and fall of your abdomen with each breath, allowing any tightness to soften.

7. Shift your focus to your chest, shoulders, arms, and hands. Notice any sensations in these areas, such as warmth, tingling, or relaxation.

8. Let go of any tension as you continue to breathe deeply.

9. Finally, bring your awareness to your neck, face, and head. Soften your jaw, relax your facial muscles, and release any tightness in your neck and scalp.

10. Allow yourself to fully inhabit your body in this present moment.

11. When you're ready, gently open your eyes if they were closed.

Listening Practice

In our overstimulated podcasted world, our capacity to truly listen often weakens rapidly. But this retrieved awareness of ambient sounds and sonic signatures is a mindfulness goldmine waiting to be rediscovered.

The practice is strikingly straightforward. First, acknowledge any rumbling thoughts or inner dialogue, then shift your focus to absorbing all the intricate sounds dancing across your eardrums. The percussion of typing, hisses of traffic in the distance, creaks of your chair, every layer reveals itself. Another profound meditation technique that involves listening is called the 5-4-3-2-1 grounding technique. It's a sensory awareness exercise that involves focusing on your senses to bring awareness to the present moment and reduce anxiety or stress.

Trust me, after returning from just 3 to 5 minutes luxuriating in these immersions, the world around you will feel exponentially more vibrant.

5-4-3-2-1 Grounding Technique

1. Find a space where you can sit or stand comfortably.

2. Take a few deep breaths, inhaling through your nose and exhaling through your mouth, allowing yourself to relax and be present in the moment.

3. Start by looking around, noticing five things you can see. These could be anything in your immediate surroundings, like a picture on the wall or a book.

4. Next, focus on your sense of hearing, identifying four distinct sounds you can hear. It might be birds chirping or the hum of appliances.

5. Shift your attention to your body, noticing three sensations you can feel: the texture of your clothes against your skin, the temperature of the air, or the sensation of your feet on the ground.

6. Pay attention to your sense of smell, identifying two different smells around you. It could be the scent of coffee or a familiar fragrance.

7. If possible, notice one taste in your mouth. Perhaps it's the lingering taste of a recent meal or simply the natural taste in your mouth.

8. Take a moment to reflect on your experience and notice how focusing on your senses brought you into the present moment and helped calm your mind.

Soundscape Soak Exercise

1. Find a space where you can sit or lie down comfortably.

2. Close your eyes to reduce visual distractions, enhancing your listening ability.

3. Take a few deep breaths, inhaling through your nose for a count of four, hold for a count of four, and exhale through your mouth for a count of four, allowing yourself to relax.

4. Begin by listening to the closest sounds. This could be your own breathing, the rustle of your clothes, or the sound of your heartbeat.

5. Gradually widen your focus to include sounds that are a bit farther away. Notice the hum of your computer, the ticking of a clock, or the soft murmur of voices in another room.

6. Finally, expand your awareness to the farthest sounds you can hear. This might be distant traffic, birds chirping outside, or the wind rustling through trees.

7. Listen to each sound without labeling or judging it. Just acknowledge its presence and let it pass.

8. After a few minutes, bring your focus back to your breath for a moment before opening your eyes.

Mantra Recitation

Even if your calendar resembles anything but a spacious oasis, the practice of silently repeating an anchoring mantra or affirmation can nourish you with vital drops of focused presence at any time.

Popular seed phrases range from the ancient "So Hum" ("I am that"/"This too shall pass") to "Breathing in, breathing out" to crafted self-talk like "I am calm, capable, and focused." Any brief chant that feels meaningful to you will work. The key is cyclically reviving your awareness each time the mind drifts from its prescribed harbor.

1. Find a space where you can sit comfortably without distractions.

2. Select a mantra that resonates with you. Any sound that holds special meaning or brings a sense of calm.

3. Sit with your spine straight but not rigid.

4. Close your eyes gently and focus your attention inward.

5. Inhale deeply through your nose, hold for a moment, and exhale slowly through your mouth to relax your body and mind.

6. Start repeating your chosen mantra either silently in your mind, softly, or out loud.

7. Focus on the sound and vibration of the mantra as you recite it.

8. Keep your attention on the mantra, allowing other thoughts to pass by without engaging with them.

9. If your mind wanders, just gently bring it back to the mantra.

10. Recite the mantra for a set time, such as 5 minutes or longer if you prefer.

11. After completing the recitation, take a moment to reflect on how you feel. Notice any shifts in your mental state or inner calmness.

Portable Zen

Do you frequently find yourself idle with bits of downtime at stoplights or in waiting rooms? It's the perfect time to spontaneously burst into some impromptu meditation practice!

This could involve fixed gaze meditation by focusing on a still object, such as a sign or a crack in the floor, and gently observing any urges to look away, or maybe you enjoy some gently guided imagery to whisk you from the physical environment into panoramic mindscapes of peaceful meadows or mountain lakes. Another option is to choose a portable object that you can easily carry with you, like a smooth stone, a small trinket, or a favorite piece of jewelry. Whatever the method, these carved-out instances become opportunities for effortlessly slipping from autopilot into presence until the externals shift again.

1. Throughout your day, whenever you feel overwhelmed, stressed, or need a moment of peace, take a mindful pause.

2. Take your chosen Zen object in your hand, or find an object to fix your gaze upon, and focus your attention on it.

3. Notice any details that stand out, engaging as many senses as possible. Listen to any sounds it makes, feel its temperature, and observe how it catches the light.

4. Take a few deep breaths, inhaling slowly through your nose and exhaling through your mouth.

5. Take a moment to appreciate the simplicity and beauty of your object. Feel gratitude for this moment of mindfulness in your day.

6. As you focus on your object and breathe deeply, allow any tension or stress to melt away.

7. Spend a few moments in stillness, simply being present with your Zen object and your breath.

8. Allow your mind to rest and your thoughts to settle.

Walking Meditation

Rather than allocate mindfulness solely to sedentary periods, why not integrate it with your body's movements? Walking meditations help you focus entirely on the amazing details of walking. You can employ walking meditation as an anchor during simple neighborhood strolls or lapping office complexes.

1. Start by finding an unobstructed path and anchor your gaze about 6 feet ahead.

2. Gently establish a slow, rhythmic stride.

3. Then, layer in conscious connectors like feeling each footfall, being aware of weight shifting subtly with each step, and noting the rise and fall of your center of gravity.

4. When you're deeply attuned, it feels almost hypnotically mesmerizing, which can make even the most familiar routes feel amazingly novel!

5. Use the steady rhythm as an impromptu metronome for checking back into embodied presence every few paces.

The Attitude of Gratitude

Gratitude listing is another great practice for a good dose of mindfulness amid chaos. This is quite literally just running a mental catalog of whatsoever you're presently appreciating or grateful for as you move throughout your day.

It could be as simple as "grateful for the verdant trees filtering sunlight through their leaves" or as profound as "appreciating the miraculous privilege of being alive and conscious." Nothing is too big or small! The act of recognizing and amplifying these felt pulses of appreciation reprograms your psychology towards optimism, beauty, and self-generating joy. Write it down, simply recite it, or do it in the shower, waiting for Uber Eats, during a hectic car service's tire rotation—whenever! Peppering spontaneous thankfulness throughout your day elevates all of your life into a delightful unwrapping of gifts.

Gratitude Moments

1. Throughout your day, pause for a few moments whenever you can.

2. Reflect on three things you're grateful for at that moment, such as the kindness of a friend, a beautiful sight, the fact that you can breathe, or a moment of peace.

3. Take a deep breath and allow yourself to fully feel appreciation for these blessings, regardless of the time of day.

4. Use these gratitude moments as reminders of the positive aspects of your life, helping you stay grounded and uplifted.

Gratitude Journaling

1. Keep a gratitude journal handy. Alternatively, you can use a notes app on your phone.

2. Whenever you have a quiet moment, jot down three things you're grateful for from recent experiences or thoughts.

3. Be specific and heartfelt in your descriptions, focusing on what brought you joy, comfort, or inspiration.

4. Return to your gratitude journal whenever you need a boost of positivity or a reminder of the good things in your life.

So, there's a sampling of mindful reinvigorators you can easily weave throughout your schedule—straightforward yet potent tools to metabolize friction and realign your bearings with the right here, right now.

Movement-Based Practices

With short, movement-based practices, like mini yoga sessions and tai chi, each movement is a dance with the air around you, where every stretch and pose unlocks a sense of relaxation and energy.

With these short sessions, you'll experience the grounding power of different poses like mountain pose, where you stand tall like a sturdy mountain, or the gentle flow of cat-cow stretch, mimicking the grace of a stretching feline. In tai chi basics, you'll flow through movements like cloud hands, embodying the fluidity of wind and water as you sway in harmony with your breath. Your limbs soften into the movements of the present moment rather than tensing against it. Each posture becomes a dance with the very oxygen surrounding you.

These mini-movement practices refresh your body and mind, the perfect remedies for an overtaxed physique and frazzled focus.

Yoga: Cat-Cow Stretch

1. Come to a tabletop position on your hands and knees.

2. Your wrists should be directly under your shoulders, and your arms should be straight. Your knees under your hips should be bent at a 90-degree angle.

3. Inhale and arch your back while lifting your tailbone and head upward, just like a cat stretching its back.

4. Exhale as you round your back, tucking your chin to your chest and your tailbone under.

5. Repeat this movement with your breath, allowing each inhale to lift and open your chest and each exhale to round and contract your spine.

Yoga: Mountain Pose (Tadasana)

1. Stand tall and with your feet hip-width apart.

2. Ground your feet into the floor and feel the connection between your soles and the earth. Think of it as roots anchoring a tree.

3. Imagine a string pulling you gently upward from the crown of your head, engaging your leg muscles and lengthening your spine.

4. Relax your shoulders and extend your arms down the sides of your body, palms facing forward.

5. Take deep, slow breaths in this pose, feeling the strength and stability of a mountain within you.

Tai Chi: Cloud Hands Movement

1. Stand with your feet shoulder-width apart.

2. Slightly bend your knees, keeping your arms relaxed by your sides.

3. Shift your weight to one leg and raise your opposite arm overhead, pretending you're scooping a cloud from the sky.

4. Slowly shift your weight to the other leg while lowering the first arm, and repeat to the opposite side.

5. Continue this flowing movement, coordinating your breath with each shift of weight and arm movement, like dancing with the air around you.

Tai Chi: Energy Flow

1. Stand with your feet shoulder-width apart.

2. Slightly bend your knees, keeping your arms relaxed by your sides, palms facing inward toward your body.

3. Slowly and steadily inhale, raising your arms to chest level, palms facing each other. Imagine you're gathering a ball of energy between your hands.

4. As you exhale, push your arms forward, palms facing outward, as if gently pressing against a resistant force.

5. Feel the energy extending from your palms.

6. Turn your palms inward again and rotate your arms outward and upward in a circular motion, as if scooping energy from above.

7. Lower your arms back down to the starting position, palms facing downward, as you bend your knees slightly, and visualize grounding your energy into the earth.

8. Repeat and Flow: Continue this flowing sequence of inhaling, raising, exhaling, pushing, rotating, gathering, and sinking for about five cycles.

These practices are easily accessible, anywhere, anytime. But let's step things a notch up and look at crafting your very own Zen zone.

I value your feedback. Please take a moment to leave an honest review, sharing your thoughts and experiences with this book.

Scan QR code to LEAVE A REVIEW

Part II:

Kick-Starting Your Quick Meditation Practice

Chapter 4:

Crafting Your Instant Zen Zone

Lose your mind and come to your senses. —Fritz Perls

When someone first suggested adding "mini-meditation breaks" into my daily grind, I internally rolled my eyes so hard I think I strained something. Like I have time between client calls and shuffling kids to each extracurricular! My perpetually starved mindshare could barely make room for another open browser tab.

I'm guessing plenty of you jugglers out there can relate. We're the gabillion-mile-per-hour multitasking mavens, careening straight from morning milkshake cleanup into the morning commute cheek-to-jowl with other hangry commuters and straight into the perpetual-motion rat race of workday demands. What if I told you that true mastery lies in conquering the illusion of "no time" and utterly obliterating the notion that any specific circumstances or environments are required? Until now, our focus has been meditation's seamless portability across even the most oversubscribed schedules, all those tantalizing tips for slipping restorative pockets of presence between work sprints, family chaos, and life's infinite contextual theatre. In actuality, the whole darn world is your personal ashram simply awaiting the activation of your attention. We're about to blow those sacred practices into an entirely new dimension of flexibility and accessibility.

The Importance of Space

Let's look at setting the sensory scene for peak mental wellness. Because the environments we consciously cultivate around us can make or break our minds and moods.

Think about it: We're smack dab in the Golden Age of dopamine-laced everything. Social media doom scrolling, binge-watching sedatives, the works. Never before have our attentions been so insidiously fragmented across a zillion simultaneous inputs and tasks. It's a veritable onslaught assaulting our nervous systems from all angles. This is precisely why intentionally curating soul-centric spaces has become so paramount for restoring equilibrium. Think of it as performing a hard reset for your frazzled psyche. Without the right environmental cues priming your subconscious for serenity, you're basically fighting an uphill battle against the surrounding digital chaos. It's not a fair fight if you ask me!

That's where the understated art of ambiance work comes in. With a few simple tweaks to what your senses are perceiving, you can hijack your physiological state from that perpetual low-key anxiety cycle. It's like a neurotransmitter hack. Some factors that come into play include:

- light
- color
- temperature
- noise
- natural elements
- personalization
- organization
- comfort

We're about to blow those sacred practices to a whole new level of flexibility and accessibility. Let's focus on the senses for starters:
- **Visual Enlightenment**
    - Natural lighting is prime for emitting those photons that nudge our circadian cycles (the natural,

approximately 24-hour rhythms that regulate physiological and behavioral processes) back on track. Welcome in as much sunbeam love as possible through your windows and skylights.

- When it comes to artificial light, invest in warm-toned bulbs or lamps that cast soothing amber glows. Avoid harsh fluorescents and blueish hues.

- Speaking of headaches, eliminate visual clutter. Process papers, wrangle kid toys, and tidy away decor vignettes for a regular, refreshing minimalist reset.

- Sprinkle in botanicals everywhere you can. Use low-maintenance succulents, trailing ivies, and cheerful florals. The organic pop of greenery is instantaneously grounding.

- **Audible Alchemy**

  - Layer in natural soundscapes to mask clanging disturbances. Create or play sounds of crackling fireplaces, gentle rain tapping, or flowing brook loop videos.

  - While words and lyrics can spike cognitive arousal, instrumental ambient playlists attenuate overthinking beautifully. Look for atmospheric genres like neo-classical, environmental music, or native flute melodies.

  - Auditory white noise can also do wonders drowning out excess commotion. Run an air purifier at high settings, or try brown noise apps that mimic a womblike thrum.

43

- On the other hand, you may discover that absolute silence provides the most profound pause for your easily overstimulated senses.

- **Environmental Choreography**

    - Enjoy the breathability of open windows, even when it's chilly out—nothing like a breath of fresh air. There's just something vitalizing about allowing outdoor air exchanges.

    - Temperature regulation is essential, too. Extreme heat or cold can cause physiological stress.

    - Experiment with different textures in your surroundings, such as smooth surfaces, rough textures, or tactile artworks. This variety can engage your sense of touch and add sensory richness to your space.

    - Assume a posture of profound relaxation rather than tolerating niggling discomforts. This may mean ergonomic cushions, zero-gravity recliners, or therapeutic massage tools peppered around on the ready.

- **Olfactory Ambrosia**

    - Invest in a quality diffuser and stock up on anxiety-melting essential oil blends. Lavender, eucalyptus, and bergamot are herbal botanic scents that act as soothing balms for our oversaturated circuits.

    - Burn purifying bundles of sage, palo santo, or sweetgrass to smudge away stagnant ions and reset energy fields.

- Unearth your favorite childhood aromas, too. Certain fragrances like coconut, fresh laundry, or banana bread can be weirdly nostalgic and cathartic for the soul.

At its core is simply being intentional about what you allow to stimulate your senses at any given time. By regulating visual patterns, soundscapes, airflow, aromas, and the like, you cultivate an environment primed to trigger the relaxation response.

Transform Any Location

We flexible-minded folks need meditation hacks that can adeptly mold to our environments and lifestyles, not the other way around. Why should decompressing from our frantic routines require extra hassle? Modern mindfulness is all about seamlessly integrating those sacred pauses into daily life. Sound too lofty a transcendence to achieve amidst all the chaos?

With a few crafty tweaks, you can curate restorative meditation spaces anywhere your crazy schedule parks you. Here's the 411 on making any scene yoga studio-worthy:

- **The Basic Bedroom**
    - Embrace minimalism, well, at least temporarily! Pack away visible clutter like that teetering laundry pile or growing "knickknack colony." Physical mess breeds mental static that can disrupt your practice.
    - Accent a cozy mood with subtle, warm lighting. String up some fairy lights, burn a softly scented candle, or open the curtains to let in natural light.
    - Bring the outdoors indoors and aim for earthy, natural accent pieces like a potted snake plant, bamboo mat, or

pile of crystals. They imbue the space with organic, grounding elements.

- Play with textured neutrals like cotton throws or faux fur pillows arranged in a makeshift meditation station. The plush, tactile textures create an aura of "This is my designated cozy zone."

- Consider introducing gentle aromas, using essential oil diffusers or sticks of palo santo to smudge stale bedroom air. Lavender and eucalyptus are particularly soothing.

- **The Family Nucleus**

    - Kids and spouses make sneaking off kind of unrealistic. But transforming a peaceful pocket of home into your refuge is completely doable.

    - If your own room isn't an option, negotiate bathroom sanctuary during set times when it's off-limits to others. Light some candles and run yourself a mindful bath.

    - If you have a covered patio or a sunny nook, cozy it up with throw blankets, pillows, and sound dampeners to claim it as your meditation sanctuary.

    - Use a hanging beaded curtain or freestanding room divider to section off a corner of any main room.

    - Establish grounding ambient noises by turning on a water fountain, looping a rain soundtrack on headphones, or guiding kids to read quietly nearby.

- **The Corporate Cubicle**
    - Claim whatever hidden nook or empty office space you can for a midday timeout. Supply closets, vacant conference rooms, or even a parked car may all become secret sanctuaries with the right tweaks.
    - Use noise-cancelling headphones or a white noise app to drown out distracting commotion, creating an instant auditory escape pod.
    - If possible, tint or adjust the lighting. Swap out harsh fluorescents for lamps with soft bulbs, or simply hang up a sheer scarf to cast a warmer glow.
    - Bring in textural and scent elements like a little plush mat and essential oil roller to re-energize your senses.
    - To drop into meditation mode faster, drape a pashmina or jacket over your shoulders and dim your screen brightness way down as a makeshift sensory deprivation solution.

- **The Outdoor Oasis**
    - Scope out secluded benches or trees in nearby parks or campus greens for some alfresco mindfulness. Prioritize shade and remove shoes for direct grass-to-skin grounding.
    - If city life is too loud, use noise dampeners like noise-canceling headphones and eye masks to visually and audibly minimize chaos.

- Open containers of essential oils like cedarwood or pine and take a couple of conscious inhales to synchronize with the outdoor aromas.

- Bring along a waterproof mat or large scarf to claim any greenery patch.

- **Micro-Meditations on Wheels**

    - Compile a "Commute Calm" playlist stocked with gently hypnotic instrumental tracks—think ambient soundscapes, guided breathwork audio, and Gregorian chant remixes.

    - Keep an essential oil roller or two in the cupholder to boost your olfactory zone.

    - Embrace the "driving meditation" by synchronizing your breath with the flow of traffic lights. Consciously inflate on the green, pause on the yellow, and fully evacuate on the red before repeating the cycle.

    - Get into the habit of punctuating transitions like entering or exiting the highway with ritualistic check-in moments.

    - During long red lights, use controlled balloon breaths to release any building tension. This pause and reset might be exactly what your body needs to calm your adrenal system.

    - Adopt the stance of punishing traffic jams as a spontaneous technology timeout rather than an impediment. Let it be a mandatory escape from being digital work fires and social FOMO (fear of missing out).

The key is to evoke tangible sensations that trigger a sense of calm and ease in your nervous system. Simple cues like muted lighting, soothing scents, plush textures, and relative silence can quickly transport you into reset mode. Of course, certain elements will feel more grounding to some than others based on personal preference. Experiment to customize your meditation oasis.

Chapter 5:

Fast-Track Techniques

The richness of present-moment experience is the richness of life itself. Too often, we let our thinking and our beliefs about what we "know" prevent us from seeing things as they really are. —Kabat-Zinn

Our bodies very much remain the terrestrial vehicles for any metaphysical exploration.

I'll never forget this one retreat I attended years back. We're talking full-tilt Bali extravaganza, the whole nine yards. I figured the fancy ashram setting would practically initiate me into my mind by osmosis.

Except on about day three, yours truly wound up with a wicked case of traveler's digestive vengeance. So much for my saintly aspirations; I could barely focus on anything beyond my gastrointestinal hell, much less some lofty meditative clarity. It was a profound reminder that no matter how enlightened our intentions are, we remain earth-merged creatures of the flesh and bone at our core.

Our awareness is inextricably rooted and filtered through these biological "spacesuits" we're borrowing. Aching, cramping, agonizing: any physical disturbances quickly disrupt our higher consciousness.

This is precisely why the body must be skillfully integrated, disciplined almost, in service of attaining unperturbable poise. We're talking deliberate alignment, dynamic micro-adjustments, and conscious breathwork to facilitate and fast-track focused clarity rather than undermining it.

So, let's delve into the mechanics of positioning yourself.

Posture, Setting, and Focus

Most of us first-time meditators start all bright-eyed and full of zeal. But then, a couple weeks in, we're squirming uncomfortably, getting incessantly distracted by ambient noise blips, and our "watching the breath" attempt devolves into mentally narrating our grocery lists.

Without crucial alignments in place, you're basically trying to defuse a ticking time bomb with a Tootsie Roll. Think I'm exaggerating? Allow me to highlight some interesting reasons why posture, surroundings, and focus are so instrumental for slipping into meditation:

- Cranial alignment (keeping your head and neck aligned) is everything. Your neck and head position directly impact the flow of spinal fluid nourishing your brain. Even slight misalignments can hinder your ability to access deeper states of relaxation and focus.

- Skeletal integrity (good posture) helps maintain your energy levels. When your bones are stacked in crystalline columns rather than hunched or splayed, your body's energy pathways can flow smoothly. Maintaining "inner elevation" is crucial for getting the most out of breathing exercises and meditation.

- Finding stability leads to calmness. Without a focal point, your senses can become restless and disrupt your concentration. "No bueno" for cultivating focus.

- Being aware of your body's signals is essential. The body's constant, unconscious physical and spatial cues can either anchor you into presence or catapult you into rumination, depending on how tuned in you are to them.

- Clarifying your intention for each meditation session can give purpose and direction to your practice. Whether it's cultivating peace, gaining insight, or simply being present, it guides focus.

- Your breathing rhythm can also profoundly impact your meditation experience. Deep, slow breaths can help calm your mind and body, while shallow, rapid breaths can indicate tension or distraction.

These aspects are all absolutely central to optimizing your brain's capability for stress release, rewiring, and insight. There's no bypassing these practicalities to earn your meditation black belt.

Fast-Track Micro-Meditation Methods

Let's transform those scattered, fleeting moments into profoundly restorative micro-meditation pit stops and look at some quick-fire techniques to snap your body, surroundings, and focused intentions into alignment.

As much as we aspire to those picture-perfect, hourlong mindfulness baths, realistically? Rather than detaching from the nitty-gritty of daily life to "meditate," these techniques can heighten your mindfulness seamlessly within the hectic ebb and flow—a few conscious breaths during the morning shower, an intentional lunchtime pause before diving back into the feed, maybe some soothing stretches while vegging out with Netflix after the kids have finally crashed.

- **Body Basics**
    - Are you clenching your jaw? Shoulders pulled up toward your ears? Perhaps your feet are contorting unnaturally? Before you assume any meditation positioning, do a full body scan to release any unconscious grips or contortions. If you notice any tension, simply relax those areas.
    - Soft eye focus is a core attentional anchor, but where you direct it makes a difference. Around eye level is

ideal for steadying your gaze without zoning out. You can also use a candle's flicker or mesmerizing object.

- Take 5 to 10 belly breaths, inhaling fully through the nose and exhaling out through pursed lips to kick your diaphragmatic flow into high gear. You can also use a visualized circuit, imagining oxygen traveling through your bodily pathways like a vibrant, vitalizing force.

- Envision two rays springing upright from the crown of your head toward the sky and simultaneously two roots unfurling from your bottom into the earth. Let this rooting and rising dynamic elongate your entire body.

- **Environmental Scene**

    - Few things yank you out of the present moment faster than wondering, "Has it been 5 minutes yet?" Take that mental labor off your plate by predefining the duration and setting a timer.

    - If you don't have a dedicated sanctuary, use noise-canceling headphones or a brown/white noise app. Earplugs plus a looped ocean or rainforest backdrop can work wonders.

    - A draped scarf, brimmed hat, or hoodie can be strategically positioned to block any excess visual stimuli and signal to your senses, "Relax time now."

    - Keep scent soothers like essential oils or potpourri sachets nearby to induce a quick aromatic reset.

    - If you don't have a cushy meditation station, scout the nearest wall, chair, floor, or nook and use props like blankets, cushions, or rolled towels to create a makeshift supported posture.

- You can ceremonially position a candle, framed mandala, potted succulent, or another micro "altar" gesture to signify, "This is a pocket of reverence I'm stepping into now."

- **Focus Frameworks**

    - Flow between different anchoring modalities at the first sign of distraction:

        - 3-5 focused breaths

        - body scan

        - visualization

        - repeat as needed

    - Mixing these up can reboot fleeting attention.

    - Sync your self-curated affirmations to movements, such as clenched fist pulses at your heart center or tracing figures on your palm.

    - Periodically pause and ask yourself, "Where is my awareness right now?" This subtle meta-awareness spark can yank you back from any mindless drifts into a refreshed presence.

    - Choose one simple sight, sensation, or prompt to be the centerpiece of your pocket practice. It could be the fluttering flame of your candle, the rise and fall of your breath, or even the hum of the AC unit. Unify all of your senses around interfacing with this sole point.

- Program mundane recurrences like hourly chimes and calendar pop-ups to automatically remind you to realign each time they're activated.

- **Technique Tips**

With this versatile artillery of quick-fire techniques at your disposal, you'll be amazed at how much tiny tweaks can amount to massive energetic upgrades over time.

By punctuating your day with these mindful micro-hits, you're also encoding your mind with a new muscle memory of attentional discipline and integrity. Each intentional gap reinforces those neural pathways, steering you straight back into the present. So, don't discount these quick-fire methodologies as somehow less legitimate than traditional marathon sits. They're simply evolved and better aligned with our rapid-fire modern flows. You're still depositing the same nutrient-rich mindfulness into your spiritual reserves, just getting awfully strategic about it.

Chapter 6:

Overcoming Time-Related Obstacles

The key is in not spending time but in investing it. –Stephen R. Covey

Between grinding at your 9-to-5, managing a household, and trying to carve out even a slice of recreational time, it can feel like there's zero room to breathe, let alone add something new to your overcrowded schedule. The idea of meditation is appealing, but who actually has the flexibility for that? Cramming in one more thing seems laughable at best. In our overscheduled, hustle-obsessed society, self-care practices often get bumped to the bottom of the priority list. Yet running on fumes without pause compromises our health, happiness, and overall quality of life.

The solution is a bite-sized meditation that seamlessly fits into your established routines. Yes, it is possible! By reframing meditation from a huge time commitment into mini mindful pauses, the obstacles dissolve. You already take breaks throughout the day—why not maximize them for your mental well-being? Finding fleeting moments of tranquility doesn't require dismantling your entire lifestyle, just a little creative application!

The Hustle and Bustle

No breaks, red-lined, pedal-to-the-metal mayhem from the moment that morning alarm blares to when you fetal position into those pillows at night. Sound familiar?

An endless slog of overcommitments, obligatory time sieves, and those insidious FOMO anxieties that keep our internal hamsters sprinting full tilt on their little wheels. What has the modern era bestowed upon us to create this state of perpetual overscheduling? Here's the full scan unveiling our era's frenzied fractures:

- **Work masquerading as a cultural identity:** These days, it's nearly impossible to draw a tidy line separating our professional lives from our personal. Technology has blurred every boundary, making our labor more of a portable lifestyle aspiration than any 9-to-5 trade transaction—one where we're conditioned to flaunt the "passion hustle" of our all-encompassing occupations.

- **A zillion open input channels:** Smartphone duties, anxious inbox tending, that endless scroll-hole of doom... our nervous systems simply weren't engineered to endure society's relentless onslaught of pinballing input at this rate.

- **A cultural metabolism at warp speeds:** Trends accelerating, news cycling, attention spans kaleidoscoping—most of us are merely scrambling to participate and process the shifts reshaping our landscapes every nanosecond. It feels like a disorienting pandemonium.

- **A terminal case of FOMO:** Thanks to algorithmically amplified distractions, we're eager to try everything that's currently popular. If we miss out on the hyped-up limited-batch concert, culinary delight, or pop-up of the moment, our experiences won't be fully rounded.

- **Programming for shiny object fixation:** Physical possessions can't even sate our dopamine addictions these days. We're conditioned to manically acquire and metabolize every headline, trending micro-drama, perspectival novelty, and identity crunch flowing past. Sadly, it's the only way our dopamine receptors can achieve peak fireworks these days.

- **A convoy of shape-shifting identities to uphold:** We're no longer afforded the luxury of embodying a singular role or track. We're simultaneously juggling our work-mode ops, fitness-influencer projections, parental obligations, and whatever buck-wild identity the social sphere is selling for the week. Massive psychic bandwidths are required for this!

- **Infrastructural hostilities everywhere:** Whether it's grappling with glitchy software, battling customer service, or cowering through that exhaust-choked freeway traffic, our routines can easily feel like an endless agility drill navigating the static life throws in our paths.

Is it any wonder we're all manically oversubscribed? Any single one of these distractions is taxing enough. Existing in these fast-paced times means our cells are bombarded by countless disruptive forces all at once. How's a seemingly well-intentioned juggler supposed to maintain any sense of calm amidst all this chaos?

Adding to this overwhelming situation, high stress levels are not just affecting our relationships and punctuality anymore. There are sounding alarms about the excessive cortisol levels speeding up

- heart disease and hypertension rates as our cardiovascular systems are pushed to the limit.

- compromised immune systems leave us vulnerable to every passing bug.

- brain degeneration and progression of dementia.

- systemic inflammation fueling joint and skin issues.

- stubborn weight gain no faddish diet can fix.

- dysregulated neurotransmitter production contributes to depression and anxiety.

- premature aging on a cellular level due to depleted stem cell reserves.

The consequences could be dire if you don't start taking back control of your schedule. You need to wake up and realize that busyness alone isn't the measure of a fulfilling life; it's like renting your happiness to a flawed algorithm.

You need to make changes to break free from this low-energy cycle and live more sustainably. The following are a couple of considerations:

- **Evaluate priorities:** Take a hard look at what truly nourishes you versus what you do out of habit or societal pressure. Whose opinions are driving your choices?

- **Learn to say no:** Every new commitment takes time away from something else. Be mindful of what you're sacrificing when you say yes without thinking. Every time you say yes to something, you're saying no to something else.

- **Reprogram your habits:** Childhood conditioning may have taught you to constantly overschedule. As a conscious adult, it's time to rewrite those patterns.

- **Set boundaries with technology:** Our devices are designed to keep us hooked. Establish clear boundaries with technology to protect your well-being.

Gaining mastery over your schedule won't happen overnight. It's a gradual process of pausing, reflecting, and renegotiating. You're essentially unlearning the unconscious productivity norms you've been relentlessly pursuing. Awareness of solutions always comes before lasting change. Consider this a wake-up call to break free from the mindless hustle. Focus on bringing presence to each moment instead of rushing through life. It's about being calm amid transitions, owning your experiences, and reclaiming your sense of self. Mindfulness becomes your ally, where you train your nervous system to stay steady and self-assured. It's about cultivating a serene presence and not allowing external pressures to dictate your inner calmness.

Strategies for Integrating Meditation

Modern life comes at us full-throttle, no doubt. But mindfulness is achievable if you get crafty about integrating it seamlessly.

I'm talking about micro-dosing those restorative awareness breaks into your current lifestyle and surroundings without arduous routine overhauls—little hacks and ritual reframes for hitting the pause button. So, let's dive into some practical approaches for making meditation mesh with your madness:

- **The 60-Second Recalibration**

    Rolling out of bed and already feeling rushed? Instead of wilding out, take a metaphorical step back with a micro meditation.

    Sit upright and simply tune into the sights, sounds, and sensations of your morning surroundings for one simple mindful minute: the quiet trill of birds, the weight of blankets draping your lap, the earthy aroma of that morning brew. This ultra-condensed snapshot of presence helps reset your body's neurochemistry from that frantic "gotta go!" program to a more grounded gear. No need to overhaul your whole routine either, these shavings of stillness fit seamlessly pre-everything.

- **While You're Waiting Mode**

    Lingering in parking lots, waiting rooms, lines, or lobbies? Rather than zoning out on your device, use those downtimes as impromptu meditation windows.

    Set a timer for 2 mindful minutes and notice the atmospheric sensations surrounding you: background hums, ambient temperature shifts, and cool air currents across your skin. Engage your senses. You can also discreetly leverage breathwork and eye-gazing techniques by centering on nearby objects like flecks in the concrete floor or ceiling tiles. Instant focus reset.

- **The "Quasi" Commute Sit**

Is notoriously bad traffic giving you grief yet again? Don't just sit there stewing; transform that vehicular vortex into a mini mobile sanctuary.

At extended red lights, close your eyes and concentrate on the sounds: horns blaring a few blocks away, the hum of your own engine idling. Better yet, sync your breathwork consciously with the flow of green-yellow-red light transitions. Get in the habit of ritualistically recalibrating yourself at transitions like on/off highway ramps, stopovers, and more. These bookend moments prime your headspace for peak focus before proceeding.

- **The Bathroom Reset**

While not the most glamorous retreat, every office or household has at least one soundproof mini-monastery available: the restroom!

Leverage those washroom interludes as excuses to ditch your devices and listen to the cadence of your own breathing for a few cycles. If no one's in earshot, you can incorporate hushed mantra repetitions, too.

Hot pro tip: Keep a discreet essential oil roller in your satchel to reset your olfactory senses if needed.

- **The Chore-Full Approach**

Need to make dinner for the fam but feeling mentally depleted from work madness? Don't just keep rallying through on vapor fumes.

Slow down and become hyper-conscious of each step as you chop, stir, or garnish. Narrate the motions in your mind's ear, like "Slicing this onion" and "Sauteing the garlic." You're encoding new neural circuits of presence. For bonus impact, incorporate some soulful rhythms as you go, swaying hips to the dishwasher's stirs or merengue pivots between the counters. Let the motions bring your full selfhood home.

And for you over-scheduled warriors familiar with shoving too many priorities into a finite number of hours? Those booked-to-the-brim vortexes can become meditation portals, too. For instance:

- **Stacked Meeting Daze**

    Keep getting swept up in a soulless succession of video chats and screen-sharing seminars? Resist the urge to multitask yourself into oblivion and choose to realign instead.

    At the start of each new engagement, pause for two conscious inhales and exhales before mentally transitioning from the previous video chat. Let the breath literally reinitiate your discernment upon arrival. You can also set a discrete timer to vibrate during longer meetings periodically and briefly close your eyes on those tones, allowing your senses to re-attune without your screen partners being the wiser.

- **Micro-Meanders**

    Overwhelmed to the point of immobility? Break that mental stagnation with a meditative twist.

    During any transitions (to the breakroom, between meetings, etc.), consciously slow your pace and hone in on your movement. Listen to the strike of each heel-toe stride unfolding, the cloth rustling, the hallways expanding before you. It's like activating "intentional walking" mode for a quick recalibration. Just a few mindful passages can transport you into anchored self-possession again.

- **Tasty Breaks**

    Are you craving a bit of downtime?

    During a hectic day of back-to-back meetings, treat your lunch break as a sacred pause. Step away from your desk, find a quiet spot, and savor each bite mindfully. Let the nourishment of your meal rejuvenate your focus and energy for the afternoon ahead.

- **Desk Focus**

    Experiencing a bit of information overload? Feeling distracted and pondering the swiftness of your attention span?

    When you're deep in focused work at your desk, use intentional breaks to reset your mind. Close your eyes for a few moments, take deep breaths, and stretch gently. You can also focus on an object while incorporating some mindful breathing. Allow your mind to rest before diving back into your tasks, enhancing productivity and mental clarity.

The busier you get, the more these microbursts of intentional presence become necessary for your holistic well-being. Those tiny recalibrations are basically reinforcing you from the inside so you can navigate harsher exterior conditions without shattering into a zillion shards. Not to mention, they integrate intentional mindfulness into even mundane daily tasks, making it more of a lifestyle principle than a separate "meditation" obligation. You're activating that higher octave of conscious awareness, not just during CrossFit sessions or those fleeting moments of manufactured retreat, but as an entire embodied way of existing through any scenario. It's a supreme self-possession where no outer turbulence can make you falter.

Obviously, mastering this level of presence takes time. Like any skill, it's a gradual layering of neural pathways through incremental repetition. But simply by incorporating bursts of mindfulness into your routine, you're steadily solidifying a new substratum of sanity.

So, check those old-paradigm notions of meditation as some time-consuming splurge at the door. This modern approach is about dissolving that compartmentalization between your "spiritual life" and regular functioning altogether. It's a 180-soul initiation to simply show up wholeheartedly to whatever arises.

Now that you understand the ins and outs of weaving your micro-meditations into your schedule, it's time to dip your toes into some stress reduction and resilience building.

Part III:
Goal-Oriented Meditation for the Busy Mind

Chapter 7:

Quick Stress and Anxiety Relief

Our anxiety does not empty tomorrow of its sorrows but only empties today of its strengths. –C. H. Spurgeon

You're stomping through the door after a rough day at work. You're frazzled, drained, and tightly wound. Every muscle in your body is coiled like a jack-in-the-box. As you peel off your shoes and slump onto the couch, you notice your heart doing a heavy metal drum roll against your ribcage. You attempt to decompress by watching TV, but your mind is a whirlwind. Looping thoughts tornado through your brain, each one competing to be the most obnoxious and persistent. "Why did I say that stupid thing in the meeting?" "How will I hit that deadline?" "Did I reply to that email?" You try taking deep breaths to settle the rising panic but to no avail. The worry keeps lapping at your mind, feeling like an unstoppable force.

In our frantic, do-it-all world, we all know the feeling of drowning in a turbulent sea of stress and anxiety. Whether it stems from work, family, finances, or just the encroaching doom-scroll of societal unrest, unchecked anxiety can wreak havoc. It ramps up cortisol levels, frays our nerves, hinders focus, sabotages sleep, and stokes an onslaught of negative emotions. Left unchecked, its corrosive effects on our mental and physical health are far-reaching. But what if you could short-circuit that stress cyclone with a few quick, strategic moves?

The New Normal?

Ah, life, a dizzying three-ring circus. It's a miracle any of us have functioning adrenal glands left. We're stressed to the max, and anxiety is our relentless plus one.

In this hyper-connected yet disconnected era, one unavoidable reality looms large: Stress isn't going anywhere. It's woven into the very fabric of modern existence. And if you don't learn to wrangle those menacing anxiety bouts, you'll end up withered in the clutches of burnout.

Why exactly is keeping your cool so crucial? Why should mastering rapid stress relief techniques be at the top of your self-care list?

- **Our bodies were not bioengineered for today's pressures:** Back in hunter-gatherer times, our stress response was a much-needed survival reflex. It prepped our ancestors to fight with or flee from beasts by pumping them full of cortisol and adrenaline. But nowadays, that same visceral reaction gets triggered by work emails and Twitter rants rather than actual life-or-death scenarios. Our bodies can't distinguish between an angry boss and an angry lion.

- **Chronic stress is Public Health Enemy #1:** When you exist in a perpetual storm of stress hormones, it turbo-charges inflammation and disrupts nearly every system in your body. Plenty of studies link it to heart disease, depression, digestive issues, sleep troubles, weight gain, accelerated aging, musculoskeletal problems, and the list goes on (*Stress Effects on the Body*, 2023)! Left unchecked, it literally rewires your brain, making you more anxiety-prone and less resilient over time.

- **We're addicted to the dopamine rush of anxiety:** Thanks to our over-taxed, multitasking lifestyles, many of us now get a twisted high from that frantic, frazzled state. Looping worried thoughts and perpetual busyness into our neurology becomes a self-reinforcing pattern that is hard-wired into our neurology. We've conditioned our brains to feel abnormally calm when operating at capacity, a dangerously slippery slope.

- **Our "grind" culture shames taking a breather:** There's this warped attitude that unless you're productive every waking nanosecond, you're failing at life. The reluctance or inability to disengage feeds into feeling constantly submerged in anxiety and overstimulation. This nonstop busyness destroys work-life balance and inner peace.

Those are just a few driving factors behind why developing stress management skills is so vital. When you can swiftly defuse anxiety at the moment and build resilience, you'll be equipped to thrive despite the demanding environment. Think of it like this: We can't control the waves of life crashing into us. But we can absolutely control how we respond to them with quick-acting techniques for hitting the pause button to give you that power.

Why Overloaded Schedules Demand Stress Relief Mastery

These days, having an overstuffed calendar is the norm—and the source of so much personal angst. We're inundated with

- push notifications zinging us into a panicked frenzy at all hours.
- the persistent itch to respond to every Slack message immediately.
- countless tantalizing distractions and time-sucks a mere thumb-tap away.
- longer hours, tighter deadlines, and ever-higher performance standards.
- blurred lines between personal and professional with WFH (work-from-home) culture.
- the creeping fear of being underpaid, underappreciated, and undervalued.
- the ultimate competitive sport of over-scheduling: parenting.

- tightly packed social calendars coordinating everyone's agendas.

- desperate attempts to "do it all" and "have it all," leaving no buffer room.

- unexpected emergencies or crises upending routines.

- tragic losses and grief punching you in the gut.

- cyclical stressors like moving, major holidays, and looming deadlines.

Feeling overwhelmed and teetering on the breakdown is pretty much the new normal. When you're sprinting from obligation to obligation, there's zero margin for error or rest. One tiny misstep and the entire rickety schedule collapses.

But, when you're ground down to dust, lacking stamina or bandwidth, that's precisely when you slip up. Your work performance nosedives, you're short-tempered with loved ones, and self-care habits careen off the rails. Suddenly, you're stuck in a draining downward spiral, making everything more difficult.

Having quick-fire techniques for pressing pause and recalibrating is your safety net. Instantaneous methods for defusing anxiety buy you a pocket of space before it escalates into a Category 5 storm. By proactively lowering your stress baseline, you'll navigate choppy waters more gracefully and resiliently.

Mastering the skills to soothe anxiety rapidly keeps you from surrendering to a tornado of racing thoughts and fidgety sensations. You'll tackle challenges with a clear head, more energy, and steady focus, staying productive and engaged. It's about developing the mental and emotional agility to roll with those churning waves, not get swallowed by them.

Beating Stress and Anxiety in the Moment

When stress and anxiety slam into you like a tidal wave, you need to be armed and ready to fight back swiftly and decisively. An arsenal of proven strategies for instantaneous relief is essential for steadying turbulent emotional waters.

These aren't vague strategies but tried-and-tested tools that trigger very specific physiological shifts in your body and brain. From neurological resets to psychology-based hacks, it's time to shut down the anxiety spiral. Get ready to learn some power moves for curbing anxiety in a few minutes flat? Let's dive in:

Progressive Muscle Relaxation (PMR)

This two-step process relieves physical and mental tension simultaneously. All it requires is to systematically tense and then relax each muscle group from head to toe. This cues your brain to more fully release holding patterns, which slashes anxiety, headaches, and insomnia and boosts feelings of control.

1. Sit or lie down and relax your body.

2. Close your eyes and scrunch up your face tightly for a few seconds, then release, relaxing your facial muscles completely.

3. Move down to your neck and shoulders. Raise your shoulders up to your ears, hold for a few seconds, then drop and relax completely.

4. Next up is your arms and hands. Make fists with your hands and tense your arm muscles, then release and relax.

5. Focus on your chest and back next, taking a deep breath in, hold it, and tighten your chest and back muscles, then exhale and release.

6. Move down to your abdomen and lower back, sucking in your stomach, hold briefly, then release and relax.

7. Finally, your legs and feet. Tense your thigh muscles by pushing your heels into the floor, hold, then release and relax.

Grounding Exercises

Anxiety puts you in a heady, spiraling state disconnected from the present. Grounding pulls your awareness back into your body and surroundings. Use grounding to engage multiple senses to cut off the anxiety loop.

1. Feel your feet firmly planted on the ground, focusing on the sensation of being rooted.

2. Take notice of textures and colors around you, engaging your visual senses.

3. Chew something crunchy and pay attention to the taste and texture as you savor each bite.

Bilateral Stimulation

These cross-body practices stimulate both hemispheres of the brain, creating an integrating effect to disrupt anxious thought patterns.

1. Sit or stand comfortably and relax your body.

2. Gently but firmly begin by tapping your right hand on your left collarbone, just below the hollow of your throat.

3. While still tapping your left collarbone, simultaneously tap your left hand on your right kneecap.

4. Alternate between tapping your collarbone and knee for a few seconds.

5. After tapping for a bit, switch sides. Tap your left hand on your right collarbone and your right hand on your left knee.

6. A simple 1–2 minutes of alternating will do the job.

7. Other options include marching in place, rolling your shoulders, or tracking an object with your eyes.

Vocal Toning

The vibration and frequency of humming or toning impact the vagus nerve and help dislodge anxiety from where it's stubbornly stuck. Try elongated exhales on a humming "mmmm" or "ah" sound.

1. Sit or stand comfortably and relax your body.

2. Inhale deeply through your nose, filling your lungs.

3. Upon your exhale, make a humming sound like "mmmm" or "ah," feeling the vibration of the sound in your throat and chest.

4. Continue humming or toning with elongated exhales, focusing on the vibration and frequency of the sound.

5. Feel free to get primal and growl or roar to release pent-up tension.

6. Allow yourself to express any emotions that arise during vocal toning, using any sound as a tool to dislodge anxiety and promote relaxation.

Mental Imagery

The incredible power of guided visualization to self-soothe triggers the relaxation response while reigning in mental chatter.

1. Sit or stand comfortably and relax your body.

2. Close your eyes and take a few deep breaths.

3. Imagine yourself in a serene setting, such as a beautiful beach, a cozy cabin in the woods, or standing near a gentle waterfall—anywhere serene.

4. Visualize the surroundings vividly, including colors, textures, scents, and sounds.

5. Vividly engage as many senses as possible: the colors, textures, scents, and sounds.

6. Allow yourself to fully immerse in the peaceful scene for a couple of minutes, letting go of any tension or stress.

Finger Counting Breaths

This is a tactile technique that combines breathing with the sense of touch to anchor you in the moment.

1. Sit comfortably with your back straight, keeping your feet flat on the floor.

2. Close your eyes and inhale deeply.

3. As you exhale, touch your thumb to your index finger, counting "one."

4. Inhale deeply again, and on the next exhale, touch your thumb to your middle finger, counting "two."

5. Continue this sequence, moving through each finger, up to "ten."

6. Repeat the cycle as needed, focusing on the sensation of touch and the rhythm of your breath.

Quick Coherence Technique

This method aligns your heart and mind, promoting emotional balance.

1. Sit or stand comfortably and place your hand over your heart.

2. Take slow, deep breaths, inhaling for a count of 5 and exhaling for a count of 5.

3. Focus all your attention on your heart.

4. As you breathe, visualize a positive feeling or memory, such as love, gratitude, or joy.

5. Continue this practice for a few minutes, inhaling the positive emotions straight into your heart and reducing anxiety.

Dancing Meditation

Dancing meditation combines free-form movement with mindfulness, allowing you to express yourself and release stress through dance.

1. Choose a piece of music that resonates with you and encourages movement. Whatever inspires you to dance.

2. Find a place where you can move freely without distractions or obstacles.

3. Begin by swaying or rocking to the rhythm of the music. Allow your body to move naturally and intuitively.

4. Focus on the sensations of your body moving to the music. Let go of any self-conscious thoughts or judgments.

5. Gradually allow your movements to become more expressive and dynamic. Use your arms, legs, and whole body to explore the space around you.

6. Keep your awareness of your body and the music, staying present in the moment. If your mind starts to wander, gently bring your focus back to the movement and rhythm.

7. As the music ends or you feel ready to stop, gradually slow your movements to a gentle sway or stillness. Take a few deep breaths and notice how your body feels.

These are just a few instant relief techniques to keep in your back pocket. But there's another key to rapidly derailing anxiety and stress: addressing it at the root psychological level:

- **Brain Dumping**

    o This act of purging swirling thoughts gets them out of your head and creates mental space to stop loops and regain equilibrium.

    o Do a mind-mapped free-write or voice recording and get it all out to get distance.

- **Worst-Case Scenario Planning**

    o This exposure therapy of sorts helps reframe unhelpful thought patterns by shining a light on the overwhelming thoughts fueling your anxiety. Surprisingly, usually, the worst case isn't as catastrophic as we envision.

    o Ask yourself: "What's the worst that can happen?" and vividly map it out.

- **Positive Reframing**

    o Identify negative self-talk loops and consciously choose a more empowering perspective to retrain stubborn, negative neural pathways.

- Make a list of reassuring coping statements to read when anxious. For instance: replace "I've totally screwed this up" with "I've got this; it's a chance to grow, so what can I learn from it?"

- **Awe Appreciation**

    - One of the quickest ways to short-circuit anxious rumination? Awe! This interrupts the brain's fear narrative by forcing your mind to "re-perceive."

    - Make a concerted effort to notice beauty or appreciate the vastness of nature. For instance: gaze up at the night sky or study the intricate veins of a leaf.

When you make these techniques a consistent habit, you build resiliency against anxiety. You'll retrain your brain's knee-jerk reactions and "cover the spread" against stressful events before they spiral. The goal? Have these powerful methods so deeply grooved into your neurology that they become your brain's default setting when pressure mounts. Like a reflex, you'll instantaneously self-correct rather than surrender to the emotional hijack. And that newfound poise and resilience? It grants you the headspace to thrive fully.

Chapter 8:

Quick Boosts for Health and Wellness

Treasure your well-being as your greatest wealth. –Lailah Gifty Akita

To be honest, how many times have you meticulously meal-prepped, hit the gym before sunrise, and guzzled enough green sludge to re-fertilize the Amazon? But despite your gung-ho efforts, your zest fizzled out like a spent sparkler. You backslid into familiar bad habits: snooze button addiction, vending machine bingeing, and an incurable case of "Netflix elbow" overtook your fleeting commitment. Your shiny new health goals lay abandoned somewhere between those good intentions and the cold, harsh reality of mustering sustainable follow-through.

We've all been there, stuck in the cycle of wanting to elevate our wellness game but struggling to make it stick long-term. One teetering stack of hurdles stands between us and cementing lasting positive change:

- our ingrained neurological patterning

- countless unavoidable stressors sabotaging our best-laid plans

- a profound lack of quick-win opportunities

Change is hard. Our brains crave the neural familiarity of existing habits, whether they're constructive or not. Every sincere endeavor to install new routines is met with psychological resistance. We're swimming against the strong currents of our own deeply grooved defaults. Healthy habits screech to a halt as primal stress responses hijack our willpower and decision-making abilities. We seek fleeting comfort in coping rituals like demolishing a tub of ice cream or doom-scrolling into oblivion.

And even when we manage to string together a few days or weeks of crushing it on the wellness front, that nagging voice of doubt sinks in: "Is this ever going to get easier?" "How long until I see tangible results?" We grow impatient in our pursuits, resigned that bettering ourselves must be this grueling exercise in deprivation and exhaustion.

That's why building in bite-sized, immediate wins is paramount to achieving meaningful, lasting lifestyle changes. When we can celebrate fast returns, it fuels our motivation and keeps us hungry for bigger, more profound upgrades. It's that crucial smash of positive reinforcement we need to override our brain's stubborn default settings and form productive new neural grooves. Quick, daily hacks, like quick meditations, that pay almost instantaneous dividends are the hot sauce that makes healthier habits irresistible! Tiny yet potent wins are our gateway, stoking our appetite for greater challenges and bolder transformations.

Redefining Health and Recovery

In today's "always-on" world, our conventional concepts of health and recovery have become inadequate, almost quaint.

Hitting the gym, practicing yoga, or taking an annual vacation can be great for a quick fix, but they don't really get to the heart of what's throwing us off balance. Like applying a flimsy band-aid to a gaping wound, these isolated efforts can't keep up with the magnitude of depleting forces we face on a daily basis. Our fundamental approach to rejuvenation and maintaining personal well-being requires an overhauled, multidimensional strategy.

Genuine health and recovery in the modern context necessitate cultivating resilience across multiple interconnected domains, not just addressing surface-level symptoms. It's about building an unshakable foundation that can handle the intense stress of our modern world through holistic, layered techniques. When these areas are strengthened, we build the resilient, full-spectrum vitality needed to thrive.

The Interconnected Pillars of Peak Human Thriving

So, just what are these key areas demanding our dedicated attention? Let's explore:

- **Physical**
  - learning to read and respond to your body's biorhythms and energy cycles
  - integrating anti-inflammatory nutrition, quality sleep, strategic movement
  - developing an attuned awareness to avoid patterns of depletion and excess
  - nurturing and honoring the body's needs

- **Cognitive**
  - strengthening executive functions like focus, working memory, and decision-making
  - expanding your window of tolerance for complexity and uncertainty
  - optimizing your capacity for innovative problem-solving and creative flow
  - training your mind's ability to find peace amidst chaos

- **Emotional**
    - deepening emotional granularity to discern subtle shifts in your internal state
    - upgrading your emotional regulation skills to release difficult feelings
    - fostering self-compassion, authenticity, and vulnerability
    - mastering nervous system self-regulation and befriending your inner critics
- **Energetic**
    - becoming attuned to your personal frequency and the energy fields around you
    - learning to create robust inner and outer boundaries
    - developing powerful energy-clearing and recalibration rituals
- **Spiritual**
    - discovering and fortifying your unique value system and moral compass
    - unearthing your life's deepest meaning, purpose, and sense of belonging
    - cultivating coherence through embodied practices unifying mind-body-spirit
    - awakening spiritually through grace and enlightenment

When these interwoven pillars are cared for, you generate uncompromising psycho-emotional and physiological resiliency. You become a shock-absorber able to roll with any punches, reinvigorating yourself after difficulties instead of succumbing to chronic depletion.

Yet our modern routines and cultural norms stand virtually opposed to developing this foundation of wholeness. The scripts around productivity, worth, and lifestyle perpetuate the very patterns causing our systemic deterioration:

- disrupted sleep patterns and desynchronized circadian rhythms
- inflammatory, nutrient-deficient diets dominating our food supply
- sedentary existences with virtually no purposeful physical exertion
- overstimulation fragments our attention and presence
- emotions judged as inconvenient and suppressed until they fester
- perpetual hustling toward ambiguous life goals without ever feeling "enough"

Essentially, we're running an unsustainable deficit across every facet of our beings—systematically leaking energy, vitality, and inner resources faster than we can replenish them. This universal syndrome of systemic depletion and exhaustion makes us profoundly vulnerable. The inevitable results? Skyrocketing rates of stress disorders, burnout, depression, metabolic disease, and immune system deregulation. We're collectively operating well below our ideal potential and birthright for thriving.

That's why transcending these dysfunctional norms through dedicated rejuvenation practices has become not just recommended but a must for staying anywhere near sustainable peak performance, emotional resilience, and physical vitality.

The Regenerative Power of Brief Mindfulness

Simply scattering modest, 5 to 10-minute routines into our daily matrix provides exponential dividends across multiple vectors. Let's recap on the benefits from a different perspective:

- **Mental Optimization**
    - heightens focus, working memory, cognitive flexibility, and decision-making
    - strengthens neuroplasticity and self-regulation over impulses and reactivity

- **Emotional Intelligence**
    - boosts self-awareness, distress tolerance, and regulation
    - heightens empathy, compassion, and our capacity for vulnerability
    - upgrades circuits for emotional processing and positive neurochemistry

- **Physiological Renewal**
    - anti-inflammatory effects protecting cells from oxidative stresses
    - lower levels of cortisol, inflammatory cytokines, and other degenerative biomarkers
    - activates the relaxation response, accelerating cardiovascular and respiratory recovery

- **Resilience and Performance**
  - soothes over-activated stress responses, calming fight-or-flight
  - replenishes psycho-emotional reserves to better withstand high-pressure scenarios
  - upgrades vagal tone, heart rate, and physiological recovery abilities

These bite-sized sessions re-instill that vital sense of presence, agency, and balance so often robbed from us.

Long-term upgrades on a biological level include:

- thicker gray matter (involved in muscle control, sensory perception, decision making, and self-control) and white matter (facilitate communication between different brain regions) insulation protecting against cognitive decline

- slower cellular aging and reinforced telomere (the protective caps at the ends of chromosomes that prevent genetic material from deteriorating) integrity

- enhanced neural network integration and overall brain optimization

- bolstered immunity and more regulated gene expression

- structural changes amplifying self-awareness and meta-cognition

Short mediations forge the type of psycho-physiological coherence and resilience required to navigate your hectic, volatile existence with a whole lot more grace.

Having these regenerative breaks offers you a powerful way to recharge. You gain the skill to consistently "come home" to your body, calm your nervous system, and stay true to your values and intentions, even amidst relentless external chaos.

Prioritizing Quality Well-Being

Sure, you make it to Friday night wobbling across the finish line. But most Saturdays and Sundays evaporate in a jet-lagged replay of catch-up chores, mindless scrolling, and sluggish recovery attempts.

That relentless cycle of running on fumes is about to end. Let's kick off by exploring a few strategies for nurturing these interconnected pillars of well-being:

- **Physical**
    - **Breathwork:** Practice coherence breathing (5 breaths in, 5 out through your nose) to realign natural rhythms.
    - **Nutrition:** Consume anti-inflammatory, nutrient-dense whole foods to fuel vitality.
    - **Movement:** Blend mobility, strength training, and grounding exercises like earthing.
    - **Body attunement:** Do body scans to receive subtle signals before burnout.
- **Mental**
    - **Meditation:** Take even 5 minutes to sharpen focus, working memory, and decision-making.

- **Neurobic exercises:** Stretch your plasticity through novel activities like brushing your teeth with your non-dominant hand.

- **Mind shifting:** Reframe challenges through journaling or talking to your "future self."

- **Digital boundaries:** Schedule tech breaks to find ease amidst the chaos.

- Emotional

  - **Self-compassion:** Talk to yourself like you would a dear friend when feeling criticized.

  - **Emotional discernment:** Label exactly what you're feeling using an Emotions Wheel.

  - **Activating calm:** Do box breathing (4 counts in, hold 4, out 4, hold 4) when anxiety spikes.

  - **The nervous system resets:** Try the shake practice or muscle tension/release routines.

- Energetic

  - **Boundary setting:** Visualize shielding yourself in a bubble of white light.

  - **Aura meditation:** Invest 5 minutes scanning and revitalizing your seven main chakras/energy points.

  - **Environmental clearing:** Open windows or use sound healing bowls.

  - **Nature attunement:** Go barefoot on grass or gaze at a body of water to re-sync.

- Spiritual
    - **Finding purpose:** Craft a personal mission statement summarizing your deepest values.
    - **Ritual and ceremony:** Celebrate sacredness through short mantras or symbols.
    - **Awe walks:** Get out in nature and allow yourself to experience its wonder.
    - **Unity moments:** Recall peak states of interconnectedness through breath and visualization.

But there's another vastly underrated ritual that, when optimized, unlocks vibrancy across every facet of your existence: sleep—the powerful regenerative force multiplier that boosts your physical, mental, emotional, and spiritual reserves.

Busy Person's Guide to Optimizing Sleep Quality

Adopting strategic, easy-to-implement routines for upgrading your sleep quality elevates slumber into something more transformative. It ignites a positive spiral, propelling you to operate at peak potential. So, let's explore why fortifying your zzz's merits is a top priority, along with some simple pre-bed rituals that take mere minutes.

Sleep Script for Anxious Rumination

1. Looping thoughts often crescendo while lying in bed, sabotaging slumber, so have a freewriting session dumping those spinning narratives onto paper.
2. Then, tear up the pages or discard the voice memo—a symbolic closure on the day.

3. Now, read any calming sleeping script out loud to re-pattern the mind (or have your phone read it back).

The Kundalini Nap

1. This yogic technique helps erase your day's stress in just 10 minutes. Lying on your back, eyes open, repeat the mantra "Hum Sa Ta Na Ma" for 5 minutes.

2. Then, follow with progressively deeper nostril breathing for another 5 minutes.

3. It triggers a deeply restorative theta brainwave state.

Legs on the Wall Pose

1. This gentle inversion pose resets your body's natural sleep-wake cycle. Simply rest with your legs up against a wall for 5–10 minutes.

2. It drains stagnant blood and cerebrospinal fluid from your brain for a reboot.

3. This is an easy way to release pent-up mental tension before slipping under the covers.

Grounding for Overactive Fight-Or-Flight

1. Lying in bed, notice your body sinking into the mattress and pillow.

2. Observe your breathing's rhythm as your belly rises and falls.

3. Feel the sensations in your limbs and each point of contact with the sheets. This re-centers your awareness in the present moment, away from spiraling thoughts.

Bathtime for Deep Parasympathetic Relaxation

1. Enjoying a hot shower or tub before bed triggers the relaxation response. Have it be a sacred, unplugged ritual with zero tech and to-do list processing.

2. Draw an organic cotton bath with Epsom salts and baking soda for remineralizing.

These are just a few A+ options for amplifying your zzz's in the time it takes to reply to a few late-night Slacks. However, getting horizontal is only half the equation for quality rest...

Optimize Your Sleep Sanctuary

- Ensure your bedroom is cool (around 65 °F), pitch black, and free of blue light.

- Ditch clock radios or anything emitting LED lights—even tiny bits are disruptive.

- Remember: an inexpensive blackout curtain or eye mask and white noise machine = game changers.

- Clear any clutter and invest in a comfy mattress and pillows to ease aches and pains.

Mind Your P.M. Consumption

- Stop eating 2–3 hours before bedtime to allow your digestion to settle.

- Avoid caffeine after 12 p.m. and limit alcohol, which disrupts REM cycles.

- Watch the timing on vitamins and supplements.

- Lay off the heavy philosophical books and films before bed (ask me about it).

Revitalizing Spray for Your Atmosphere

- Spritz some diluted lavender essential oil around your bedroom.

- Its calming fragrance lowers heart rate, eases anxiety, and prepares for rest.

- Consider upgrading to an essential oil diffuser humidifier for added serenity.

By integrating these strategic micro-practices into your daily flow, you'll experience exponential full-spectrum rejuvenation. Sleep's regenerative alchemy, powered by mindfulness and holistic self-care, will undoubtedly propel you into sustained peak vitality. Each night's rest manufactures mental clarity, emotional resilience, and energetic vibrancy. You'll show up fully nourished and present for any role you're required to step into.

Speaking of which, we can now explore cutting-edge strategies for magnifying your work efficiency and amplifying creativity to bring your boldest visions to fruition.

Chapter 9:

Boosting Work Efficiency and Creativity

So much of our work amounts to the drudgery of arranging means toward ends, mechanically placing the right foot in front of the left and the left in front of the right, moving down narrow corridors toward narrow goals. Play widens the halls. Work will always be with us, and many works are worthy. But the worthiest works of all often reflect an artful creativity that looks more like play than work. –James Ogilvy

How many times have you slumped back from your desk, feeling like a deflated balloon animal from a kid's birthday party? Depleted, disengaged, questioning if any of it even matters.

Whether punching the clock at an office cubicle farm or leading the C-suite brigade at a high-rise megacorp, that soul-suckingly profound sense of "Is this really it?" eventually comes for us all. Those flashes of existential dread cut straight through the monotony and cookie-cutter routines. Even for passionate entrepreneurs and trailblazing innovators, the thrill can start feeling more like billowing burnout smog. What once sparked inspiration now feels like a tired routine. Maybe you've convinced yourself this dissatisfaction is just the price for status or stability. You've grown accustomed to sleepwalking through autopilot, operating as a zoned-out drone rather than firing on all cylinders. Despite all your professional accolades or entrepreneurial accomplishments, you've been functionally trapped.

Here's the unfortunate plot twist: That dull feeling of disillusionment isn't inevitable. It's a code red that you've been holding back your potential rather than unleashing it.

Innovation, creativity, and productivity aren't just buzzwords. They're the key to meaningful achievement and fulfillment. When you lose touch with these, everything shrinks. Your sense of purpose and progress fades until you feel stuck and purposeless. You become bitter and cynical.

But using creativity and productivity as driving forces? That's how leaders and innovators expand their impact. That energy helps us overcome inertia and break through limits. When you embrace your creative energy and combine it with effective action, you gain the power to accelerate your career and master your life. Desires are reignited, limits are shattered, and new opportunities open up. Activating this potential wakes you up from autopilot.

Unmasking Workplace Burnout

A sinister force has taken hold, eroding the souls of employees across industries and positions. This force is burnout—a state of chronic stress, emotional exhaustion, and disillusionment that has become a hallmark of our time.

The foundations upon which our workplaces are built have become fertile ground for the seeds of disengagement, disillusionment, and a profound loss of purpose to take root.

The Unrelenting Pace: When Productivity Becomes a Pitfall

At the core of burnout lies an unrelenting, merciless pace that has become the norm in countless organizations. Employees are expected to operate at maximum capacity indefinitely, shouldering incessant workloads and grappling with unrealistic deadlines. The constant influx of emails, meetings, and digital distractions creates a state of perpetual overwhelm, leaving little room for focused, meaningful work. In this high-stress environment, the pursuit of ever-greater productivity and optimization often comes at the cost of quality, creativity, and personal fulfillment.

- The deluge of tasks and responsibilities is unceasing, with no respite in sight, leading to a sense of being perpetually behind and inadequate.

- The barrage of digital communication and notifications contributes to a state of constant distraction, fragmenting attention and impeding deep work.

- The relentless drive for efficiency and streamlining processes can inadvertently stifle creativity and innovative thinking, as employees are reduced to cogs in a well-oiled but soulless machine.

- The pressure to continuously outperform and deliver more with fewer resources breeds a culture of overwork and unsustainable expectations.

The Autonomy Deficit: Micromanagement's Insidious Impact

In the pursuit of control and uniformity, many organizations have embraced a management style that prioritizes excessive oversight and rigid hierarchies. While intended to promote efficiency, this approach often has the unintended consequence of stifling employees' sense of agency and control over their work. This lack of autonomy breeds disengagement, as employees feel like cogs in a machine rather than valued contributors.

- Stringent policies and procedures, while well-intentioned, can discourage innovation and creative problem-solving, as employees are forced to operate within narrow confines.

- Micromanagement and constant scrutiny breed resentment and a sense of being distrusted, eroding motivation and job satisfaction.

- Rigid hierarchies and top-down decision-making processes can leave employees feeling powerless and disconnected from the organization's broader mission and vision.

The Stagnation Trap: When Growth Stalls, Motivation Wanes

Repetitive tasks and monotonous routines can dull the senses and kill intellectual curiosity. At the same time, a lack of meaningful challenges or opportunities to grow can erode motivation and a sense of purpose.

- The absence of clear pathways for growth and upward mobility can breed a sense of being stuck in a professional rut, leading to disillusionment and apathy.

- Highly specialized roles or narrowly defined job descriptions can limit exposure to new challenges and diverse experiences, stifling personal and professional growth.

- Feeling undervalued or unappreciated, particularly in roles with limited recognition or reward structures, can breed resentment and a sense of futility.

- The lack of intellectual stimulation and opportunities to learn and expand one's skillset can quickly lead to boredom and disengagement.

The Culture of Overwork: Blurring the Line Between Job and Identity

The glorification of long hours and an "always-on" mentality has created a toxic, unsustainable, and unhealthy dynamic. Employees feel pressured to prioritize work over personal life, leading to imbalance and resentment. When work becomes the primary source of identity and self-worth, burnout becomes an existential crisis.

- The implicit or explicit expectation to be available and responsive at all hours, enabled by technology, has blurred the boundaries between work and personal life.

- The perception that one's value is measured by the number of hours logged or the extent of personal sacrifice for the job can breed unhealthy obsession and self-neglect.

- The constant need to prove one's commitment and dedication through extended hours and weekends can lead to a vicious cycle of overwork and diminishing returns.

- The pressure to conform to an idealized image of the "hard-working, dedicated employee" can breed resentment and disillusionment when reality fails to match the romanticized notion.

The Toxicity Factor: Unhealthy Workplace Dynamics

Dysfunctional team dynamics, office politics, and interpersonal conflicts can create a hostile and draining environment, sapping energy and motivation from even the most dedicated employees.

Bullying, harassment, and discrimination take a heavy toll on mental health and engagement, while a lack of trust, transparency, and open communication breeds insecurity and resentment.

- Toxic workplace relationships, whether with colleagues, subordinates, or superiors, can create a constant state of stress and emotional strain.

- Gossip, backstabbing, and political maneuvering can breed a climate of mistrust and paranoia, diverting energy from productive work.

- Discrimination, harassment, and marginalization based on factors such as gender, race, age, or disability can create a hostile and demoralizing environment.

- Lack of clear communication and transparency from leadership can breed speculation, rumors, and a sense of being kept in the dark, further eroding trust and engagement.

The Societal Pressures: Navigating Unrealistic Expectations

Beyond the confines of the workplace, societal pressures and expectations can also contribute to the burnout epidemic.

The pursuit of success and material wealth, often defined by narrow and unrealistic standards, can create dissonance and disillusionment when these goals fail to bring the promised fulfillment. The constant comparison to others' curated online personas can breed inadequacy and diminish self-worth.

- Societal fixation on conventional markers of success, such as wealth, status, and power, can lead to a disconnect from one's true passions and values.

- The pressure to conform to narrow definitions of "achievement" and "success" can breed disillusionment and a sense of failure, even in the face of considerable accomplishments.

- The constant exposure to carefully curated online personas and highlight reels can foster unrealistic expectations and a sense of inadequacy as one's own lived experience fails to measure up.

- Pursuing external validation and societal approval can lead to a loss of authenticity and a disconnect from one's true aspirations and motivations.

The Psychological Toll: When Burnout Becomes a Vicious Cycle

Burnout beyond the workplace, seeping into every aspect of life and perpetuating a vicious cycle of physical, emotional, and cognitive impairment. Chronic stress and exhaustion can lead to cognitive deficits, further compounding the challenges of navigating a demanding work environment.

- Emotional depletion can manifest as cynicism, detachment, and a loss of empathy—straining personal and professional relationships and contributing to a sense of isolation.

- Physical symptoms, including headaches, sleep disturbances, weakened immunity, and potentially more severe health issues, can exacerbate burnout and impair overall well-being.

- The psychological toll of burnout, including increased risk of anxiety, depression, and other mental health issues, can create a self-perpetuating cycle, making it increasingly difficult to cope with stress and maintain a healthy work-life balance.

The consequences of burnout extend far beyond the workplace, seeping into every aspect of life. Relationships suffer as emotional resources dwindle, and personal dreams and aspirations take a backseat, leaving people feeling trapped and unfulfilled. Unless you confront and address the myriad factors contributing to this crisis, the toll on individual well-being and organizational productivity will only continue to mount.

Mindfulness Hacks for the Workplace to Boost Productivity and Innovation

Rife with distractions, high-stress situations, and cognitive overload—the perfect ingredients for scattered, frazzled minds and suboptimal performance. Welcome to the modern workplace.

However, an increasing body of research points to mindfulness meditation as a powerful antidote to these workplace challenges. A study published in 2020 found that employees who participated in a workplace mindfulness program reported significant reductions in perceived stress and improved ability to stay focused under pressure (Brinkmann et al., 2020). Similarly, another study published in 2008 demonstrated that just brief loving-kindness meditations boosted participants' sense of social connection and positive emotions towards colleagues (Fredrickson et al., 2008).

When you pause and turn your gaze inward, even for a few minutes, you create space to observe the workings of your mind with greater clarity and objectivity. This heightened self-awareness is the foundation upon which personal growth is built. Beyond fostering personal growth, regular meditation practice also cultivates a profound sense of empathy—the ability to understand and share the feelings of others.

Let's take a look at how you can transform your workday with mini-meditation breaks:

Body Scan for Creativity

Before diving into a project that requires innovative thinking, take a few moments to tune into your physical sensations through a body scan meditation.

This practice has been shown to stimulate the brain's default mode network, which is associated with mind-wandering and spontaneous insight. A study published in the *Neuroreport* journal found that participants who engaged in a body scan meditation before completing a task showed heightened activity in the brain regions involved in attention, interception, and sensory processing—capacities that are essential for original ideation (Lazar et al., 2005).

Bring your attention to the sensations in your body, systematically scanning from the soles of your feet up to the crown of your head, remember? Note areas of tension or relaxation without judgment. This process of focused attention and present-moment awareness can prime your mind for greater creativity and problem-solving capacity.

Breath Awareness for Focus

For a wandering mind, gently redirect your attention to the simple sensation of inhaling and exhaling.

Mindful breath practice calms the nervous system's fight-or-flight response that workplace stressors can trigger. Whether you're tackling a complex task or sitting through a lengthy meeting, breath awareness can be a powerful tool for maintaining concentration and presence. In 2016, research published in the journal *PLOS ONE* showed that engaging in mindful breathing for just a few minutes enhanced participants' capacity to foster positive automatic thoughts significantly, leading to a notable reduction in anxiety levels (Cho et al., 2016). With a more regulated physiological state, you'll find it easier to remain focused and engaged, even during mentally taxing periods.

Mindful Listening for Effective Communication

It's all too easy to find ourselves formulating responses while others are still speaking, missing crucial pieces of information.

This is where mindfulness comes in; it alters your general state and receptiveness to incoming stimuli. A study published in the *Consciousness and Cognition* journal found that participants who engaged in a brief mindfulness induction were more aware of surprise distractions (Schofield et al., 2015). So, being mindful might help you notice unexpected things better (so you don't miss them).

Before engaging in an important conversation or meeting, set the intention to listen deeply without the constant internal narrative of planning your next comment. When you notice your mind wandering, simply return your attention to the speaker's words and the act of listening itself. This will foster greater empathy, understanding, and collaborative problem-solving.

Nature Breaks for Stress Relief

Taking a brief nature break can be a powerful way to reset and recharge during a demanding workday.

A study published in *Frontiers in Public Health* revealed that just 15 minutes of walking in nature lowered cortisol (the stress hormone) levels significantly (Kobayashi et al., 2019). Even if it's just a short walk around the block, intentionally attune your senses to the sights, sounds, and smells of the natural world. This practice of mindful nature connection has been shown to reduce stress, anxiety, and rumination while boosting mood and cognitive performance. Periodically stepping away from the artificial confines of the office will enable you to return to your tasks with a refreshed perspective and renewed vitality.

Mindfulness in Meetings

Meetings can be notorious for mind-wandering and disengagement. Research findings indicate that over time, people's attention tends to drift, regardless of the complexity of the task, eventually reaching a 50% distraction rate by the end of the activity (Zanesco et al., 2024).

Try incorporating brief mindfulness practices at the start or during transitions to counteract this tendency. For example, you might begin by inviting all participants to take three conscious breaths together, anchoring their attention in the present moment. Or, during a lull in the conversation, you could guide a minute of silent awareness, allowing everyone to reset and re-engage more fully.

Practical Workplace Meditation Tips

- Set reminders or alarms to prompt mindful breaks every 90 minutes. This is a great cycle for sustaining peak productivity.

- Lead by example and share mindfulness techniques with colleagues to create a more present, focused, and compassionate work culture.

- Find a quiet space, even if it's just a corner of the office or an unused conference room. Consider suggesting "mindful zones" where employees can retreat for meditation.

- Keep practices brief; even 5–10 minute micro-meditations can yield great cognitive and emotional benefits.

- New to meditation? Ease in with shorter 2–3 minute practices until you build familiarity with the techniques.

- Be patient and persistent; the benefits of meditation tend to accumulate gradually over consistent practice.

- Consider more structured options like weekly lunchtime meditation sessions or an app-based program like Headspace or Calm for added accountability.

- Create sensory kits with essential oils, textured objects, or calming music for sensory-focused meditation breaks.

- Practice mindful eating during lunch. Savor each bite, paying attention to your food's flavors, textures, and aromas.

- Cultivate a positive and encouraging inner dialogue to support your meditation practices.

- Take regular breaks from screens to rest your eyes and mind. Use this time to practice mindfulness, focusing on your breath or the sensations in your body.

- Establish phone-free times in the office to encourage face-to-face interactions and reduce digital distractions.

What to Avoid

- Avoid multitasking during meditation breaks. This negates the benefits of present-moment focus.

- Don't judge distracting thoughts or physical sensations. Simply notice them with friendly awareness and return to your anchor.

- Stop forcing extended meditation sessions when time is limited. Remember, shorter bursts are just as effective!

- Refrain from overthinking meditation techniques or trying to perfect every aspect of your practice. Allow yourself to explore different methods and find what works best for you without getting caught up in excessive analysis or self-criticism.

- Try to not become attached to specific outcomes. Approach mindfulness with an attitude of curiosity rather than striving for perfection.

In a culture that often glorifies burnout, constant busyness, and successism, these intentional meditation breaks are potent reminders to pause, breathe, and reconnect with the present moment. By thoughtfully integrating these evidence-based mindfulness hacks into your workday, you'll be cultivating the essential capacities of self-awareness, emotional intelligence, and empathy that allow you to show up as your best self, both professionally and personally.

Chapter 10:

Cultivating Personal Growth in Limited Time

An awake heart is like a sky that pours light. –Hafiz

The bings and buzzes of notifications were deafening, vying for my attention. My mind, once a vast, tranquil landscape, now resembled a juggling act in perpetual disarray as I frantically triaged emails, messages, and endless digital inputs.

In that moment, I was acutely aware that something profound had been lost amidst the frenzy, a sense of being present, of savoring each fleeting experience fully before it dissolved into the next urgency. It was then that my gaze landed upon a simple ceramic bowl perched atop my cluttered desk, a relic from a bygone era when life moved at a more grounded pace. Cradling it in my palms, I was transported to the memory of watching its maker, a seasoned potter, effortlessly shaping the malleable clay with calloused yet masterful hands. In stark contrast to the feverish multitasking that had become my modus operandi, the potter's art was an ode to patience, presence, and growth, an honoring of the truth that profound transformation arises not through frenzied effort, but by attuning to the sacred rhythm of life itself. I was reminded of the beauty that blossoms when we surrender to the journey rather than merely fixating on the destination.

How often do we truly lean into this fertile process of becoming rather than unconsciously striving, clinging, and repressing our way through the richness of each day?

At that moment, with the humble ceramic bowl, I recognized that the most essential ingredients for real personal growth and empathy cultivation are obscured by the urgencies that consume us. By continually operating in a state of reactivity and distraction, we deny ourselves the opportunity to turn our gaze inward with acceptance and patience. We neglect the sacred pauses that allow us to gently greet our own vulnerabilities and struggles.

It is this opening of the heart, this willingness to embrace your full and imperfect self, that awakens your capacity for growth.

The Untapped Catalysts: Self-Awareness and Empathy

In our go-go-go world, we're all crazy busy, responding to the latest fire drill and checking boxes to power through our massive to-do lists.

But if you're not careful, you can easily lose sight of what really matters: your own personal growth and capacity for understanding others. Without intentionally developing your self-awareness and emotional intelligence, you'll remain stuck on the hamster wheel, lacking the mindset and human skills to show up as your best version every day. What's the deal? Why does this inner work around personal growth and empathy matter so much?

For starters, it's the secret that unlocks your ability to innovate and develop creative solutions. Sure, frameworks and methodologies have their place. But the freshest thinking emerges when you take the time to understand yourself and your inner workings at a deeper level. Think about it: When was the last time you had a brilliant idea? Chances are it didn't strike like a lightning bolt but arose from a period of reflection and open-minded exploration. Maybe you were taking a shower, going for a walk outside, or just staring off into space, allowing your mind to wander freely. In those calm, quiet moments, you were able to shed the blinders of your usual thought patterns and assumptions to perceive things from a fresh vantage point.

That's true creative thinking: stepping out of the hustle to consciously explore your inner terrain without judging or shutting anything down. It's developing the self-awareness to recognize your blind spots, fears, and limiting beliefs so you can move beyond them.

It's more than just thinking up the next big thing, though. It's also a key factor in developing resilience, emotional intelligence, and strong relationships:

- When you take the time to tune into your thoughts, feelings, and reactions, you build valuable emotional awareness. You become better equipped to understand what's driving you, manage your state, and remain levelheaded in tough situations instead of getting hijacked by your mood.

- Exploring your inner world with curiosity and self-compassion fosters a deep sense of self-acceptance. You come to embrace all parts of yourself, strengths and weaknesses, rather than brutal self-criticism. This boosts confidence and authenticity.

- Connecting with your emotional reality helps you relate to what others are experiencing. When you can put yourself in someone else's shoes and empathize with their perspective and feelings, you become a much better listener, collaborator, and leader.

Personal growth and empathy skills don't just benefit you on an individual level. When it comes to improving teamwork, communication, and innovation, they're game-changers:

- Having self-aware members (whether family, friends, or colleagues) who can regulate their emotions creates an environment of trust, collaborative problem-solving, and productive conflicts where everyone feels safe to voice their views.

- Tapping into different experiences and viewpoints sparks new creative possibilities and solutions that expand beyond any one person's insular way of looking at things.

- Practicing empathy and really striving to understand diverse perspectives allows groups to be more solution-driven, leading to happier, more fulfilled outcomes.

- Leaders who exemplify emotional intelligence, self-awareness, and empathy engage others at a deeper level and inspire a stronger sense of fulfillment and meaning.

At the end of the day, we're all human beings, not machines or resources. When we make space to honor our inner experience and share that level of vulnerability and understanding with others, we form bonds that unite us in our shared hopes, fears, and desires. From that place of connectedness, we're capable of so much more innovation, productivity, and impact.

Awakening Through the Moments: Embedding Mindfulness

We all know that making time for personal growth, self-reflection, and developing a deeper sense of empathy would be beneficial. But realistically, when you're slammed with a million things on your plate, who has hours to spend?

You don't need huge chunks of time to start cultivating more self-awareness and making strides in your personal transformation journey. Those precious small pockets of time intentionally throughout your day can make serious progress in getting to know yourself better and expanding your capacity for understanding others. Brief mindful moments (whether it's a few deep breaths at your desk, a short meditation while waiting for your coffee, or an intentional pause to check in with your emotions and thoughts) act as small interruptions that shake you out of autopilot. Over time, this accumulates into expanded emotional intelligence, increased empathy, restored balance, and new insights that can catalyze growth in all areas of your life.

Here's how to start taking advantage of these "micro-opportunities" for personal development:

At Your Desk or Work Station

- **Do a body scan:** Our familiar go-to. Take 2–3 minutes to bring your awareness into the present. Remember, simply observe with curiosity where you might be holding unnecessary stress or tension.

- **Check in with your emotions:** Periodically ask yourself, "What am I feeling right now?" Then, allow yourself to sit with that emotional experience for a moment with curiosity and acceptance. Don't try to change it; simply notice the quality of the emotions arising. This builds emotional literacy.

- **Practice mindful breathing:** When you start feeling scattered, anxious, or frazzled, pause and bring your full attention to the simple process of inhaling and exhaling for 60 seconds. This activates your body's natural relaxation response.

Pro tip: Set a calendar reminder to pause for these mini-mindfulness breaks 2–3 times per day, especially before diving into something important, stressful, or creative. Consciously let go of whatever you were working on to be fully present.

What to avoid: Don't get hijacked by your thoughts and slide into damaging self-criticism or rumination if you notice difficult emotions or harsh self-judgment. The aim isn't to change anything but simply to observe your internal experience with friendly curiosity and self-compassion.

While Commuting or Running Errands

- **Check in with your senses:** While walking or driving, take a moment to notice the sights, sounds, and smells around you with fresh perception as if experiencing them for the first time. Let your eyes linger on the scenery without mentally narrating. This pulls you out of your head.

- **Practice listening:** If you're with someone or on a call, bring your complete attention to not just their words but their tone, emotion, facial expressions, and body language. Suspend any urge to plan your reply; just listen deeply and imagine yourself in their shoes.

- **Tune into your body:** Notice your posture, pace, and breathing pattern as you move through your day. Are you tensing your shoulders without realizing it or holding your breath? Relax and find a healthy, grounded rhythm. Consciously smooth out any areas of unnecessary contraction.

Pro tip: Treat transitions like stopping at red lights or waiting for the train or elevator as opportunities for these micro-mindful check-ins. The smaller the window, the better you'll get at shifting into presence quickly and easily.

What to avoid: Don't multitask while also attempting to be mindful. Anytime you find yourself flipping between tasks, take that as a signal to simply drop back into focused presence on whatever you're doing at that moment.

In Meetings or Group Settings

- **Open group meditation:** Before diving into the discussion, guide others through 2–3 minutes of guided breathwork, a body scan, or a short centering practice to become grounded and present. Give people permission to let go of what they're working on.

- **Engage your empathy:** As others speak, periodically put aside your mental commentary, agenda, and inner responses. Instead, imagine yourself fully in their shoes, feeling what they feel and seeing through their lens of perception without judgment.

- **Notice group dynamics:** With an objective, curious, and nonjudgmental mindset, observe communication styles, power dynamics, and areas of tension or cohesion. Where are allies being formed? What's being avoided or causing friction? These insights can inform better facilitation and results.

Pro tip: If everyone is open to it, volunteer to start or close meetings and gatherings with a short mindfulness prompt or moment of silence. Leverage "lead by example" and model being the grounding force and inlet of calm if others get frenzied, escalated, or hijacked by reactivity.

What to avoid: Jumping immediately to judgments, evaluations, or formulating your counterpoints and solutions as others speak. Simply observe the human experience unfolding in the room with acceptance, openness, and care first.

In Moments of Downtime or Transition

- **While waiting:** Instead of pulling out your phone or computer, pause and breathe deeply. Take in your surroundings with full presence: the sounds, smells, and feeling of the air on your skin. There is no need to narrate or evaluate your experience.

- **During chores,** Bring your full loving attention to routine tasks like washing dishes, folding laundry, cleaning, or pulling weeds. Use the tasks as anchors for present-moment awareness to find the meditation in these mundane moments.

- **When waking or going to bed:** Start and close each day by checking in with your emotional state and bodily sensations and setting an intention for self-care or extending compassion as you move through your day. There is no need to overcomplicate it.

Pro tip: Get an app or wearable device or set a repeating phone reminder to prompt you to drop into a 2-minute breathwork, intention-setting, or mindful awareness practice several times each day.

What to avoid: Stop treating these downtime pockets as a chance to multitask, check emails, or consume content quickly. Be intentional about using them just for you to recharge, reset, and embody presence.

The Benefits Compound Over Time

At first, making space for these ultra-mini mindful moments may feel awkward, uncomfortable, or forced. You might notice a constant urge to get back to work or feel like you're unproductively wasting time. But as the habit of pausing and re-centering solidifies, the impacts will begin to amplify in profound ways:

- You'll develop a keener emotional awareness and ability to self-regulate on the fly. With practice, you'll be able to catch yourself before getting hijacked by difficult emotions, keeping you resilient and level-headed even in stressful situations.

- Getting frequent neutral, third-party perspectives on your inner experience, tendencies, and knee-jerk reactivity makes it easier to pinpoint your blind spots and override destructive thought patterns before they take over.

- Practicing empathy for others consistently, even in small ways throughout your day, strengthens those "muscles" for perspective-taking. You'll gain a greater understanding and make better connections during bigger discussions, negotiations, or conflicts.

- Tuning into the present through your senses and breath pulls you out of excessive rumination over the past or catastrophizing about the future - two guaranteed ways to amplify anxiety and separation from what's actually happening here and now.

- These tiny pauses throughout each day prevent you from operating solely on autopilot and unconscious conditioning. You'll feel more engaged, intentional, and attuned to the richness and fullness of your life unfolding.

- Ironically, being more wholly present in your direct experience allows you to accomplish more by giving your full attention to one thing at a time instead of constantly partial "monkey mind" amid multitasking.

The wonderful thing about embedding personal growth practices into your existing routines and transition periods is that it doesn't require radically disrupting your current lifestyle or cramming major events into an overwhelming schedule. You can start exactly where you are, incrementally building up your self-awareness, empathy capability, and capacity for meaningful change. You no longer have to feel guilty or perpetually fall short because you "don't have time" to go deep into self-work.

If You Liked This Book, You Might Also Like…

Part IV:

Integrating Mindfulness Into Your Daily Routines

Chapter 11:

Making Meditation a Seamless Part of Life

Altogether, the idea of meditation is not to create states of ecstasy or absorption but to experience being. –Chögyam Trungpa

The simple act of breathing, in and out, is the most fundamental rhythm that unites all living beings across this vast universe.

As my awareness descended into the warmth of my oatmeal bowl cradled between my hands, the maelstrom of looping thoughts and mental chatter receded like clouds parting to unveil a brilliant blue sky. Suddenly, the humble bowl before me revealed itself as a doorway into the very essence of existence itself. I rooted my senses fully, the nutty aroma wafting upward, the subtly shifting hues and textures as the oats cooled, the fleeting sweetness across my tongue. What had previously been a rote, barely conscious activity came alive in high definition. I surrendered into this domain of pure presence—no past, no future, just the perfection of one breath flowing into the next within the sacred mundanity of breakfast. It was an experience that has unfolded billions of times yet never quite like this. All illusions of separation between self and world momentarily dissolved.

While savoring breakfast is hardly a revolutionary spiritual practice, the profound truth it reminded me of continues to resonate deeply each time I remember to drink from its simple wellspring: that living meditatively, with exquisite all-encompassing awareness, doesn't require splendid vistas or silent monasteries. The opportunity to awaken the sacred within the mundane lies within every ordinary breath and everyday moment. It simply takes the courage to show up fully and to shed deeply entrenched habits of critique and inattention, to look upon the most basic aspects of human existence not through the alienated fog of conditioning but with authentic curiosity, acceptance, and a beginner's mind.

The portal to awakening has always been here. Every morsel of your life is calling you to savor its wholeness from the inside out.

Sense and Sensibility: Multitasking

The concept of multitasking has become a pretty standard ingredient in our cultural fabric. We applaud those who can juggle multiple priorities simultaneously, seeing it as a hallmark of productivity and skill.

This mindset of constantly task-switching between workflows, conversations, and inputs may not be as efficient or effective as we've been conditioned to believe. While multitasking can sometimes be unavoidable in today's fast-paced environments, the reality is that our brains are essentially single processors when it comes to cognition and focus. It's no secret that intensely focusing on one task at a time yields higher productivity, accuracy, and retention compared to multitasking.

- A University of London study found that participants who multitasked during cognitive exercises experienced IQ scores decline similar to those induced by smoking marijuana or pulling an all-nighter (Will Knight, 2005). Ouch!

- Further research published in the *Proceedings of the National Academy of Sciences* showed that heavy multitaskers are actually worse at filtering out irrelevant information and exhibit diminished cognitive abilities (Ophir et al., 2009).

Rapidly switching between tasks and information streams creates start-up and lag time as the brain reorients itself each time, significantly decreasing overall efficiency. Logical, right? The novelty of constantly juggling different inputs triggers a dopamine reward loop that can be highly addictive. However, beneath that veneer of busyness lies compromised depths of thinking, increased mistakes, lack of presence, and impaired ability to process information at a deeper level. But when does multitasking make sense?

While extensive multitasking carries productivity costs, there are certainly scenarios where moderate task-switching can serve you well, including:

- repetitive or passive activities that don't require intense focus, like commuting, doing chores, or exercising (Multitasking by listening to podcasts or audiobooks falls into this category.)

- creative brainstorming and open-ended thinking, allowing your mind to wander between different ideas and thought threads, can spark new insights

- quickly context-shifting between defined, compartmentalized tasks for short bursts, which can actually boost engagement and provide a sense of progress

The key factor is balancing multitasking tendencies with dedicated periods of sustained, distraction-free concentration to tap into our brain's peak cognitive capabilities.

Why Mindfulness + Routine Tasks = Productivity Boost

While combining multiple complex activities like writing reports and taking phone calls is the type of multitasking that sabotages focus and effectiveness, an intriguing paradox emerges when we layer mindfulness practices onto our routine, habitual daily activities like:

- walking
- eating
- showering
- commuting

- doing household chores

Far from detracting from productivity, bringing a gentle mindfulness lens to these mundane moments enhances cognitive functioning, emotional regulation, and overall well-being. Here's why:

- These common activities are so habituated and routine that little active thinking is required to execute them. Our brains automatically cycle through the motions on autopilot with little present awareness.

- By consciously anchoring your attention on the felt sensations of these experiences as they unfold, you're exercising your mindfulness capacities while simultaneously allowing space for spontaneous insights, creative perspectives, and mental recovery to arise naturally.

- Routine tasks like walking provide the perfect "neutral" backdrop to simply notice your breath, bodily sensations, emotions, and thought patterns in a detached yet intimate way, sharpening your self-awareness and equanimity muscles.

- Rather than zoning out or fueling restlessness by layering another cognitive activity on top, mindful attention during mundane tasks allows your cognitive resources to recharge while paradoxically cultivating presence.

You're transforming activities that would typically be reactionary muscle memory into proactive mindfulness training.

So, how is it different from multitasking?

While it may sound counterintuitive, combining mindfulness practices with routine behaviors like these is fundamentally different from multitasking.

Here's why:

- You're fully engaged in the task at hand rather than splitting attention. The mindfulness component is refocusing your awareness of the experience itself.

- There's no competing concentration required, no toggling between disparate inputs. You simply notice the sensations, thoughts, and feelings that naturally arise.

- Your attention isn't fragmented, and multitasking doesn't drain available cognitive resources. Mindfulness allows you to replenish and sync those resources.

- You're training your brain's stamina for undivided presence rather than constantly reinforcing restlessness and partially distracted focus.

At the end of the day, productive mindfulness during routine tasks allows you to be more fully immersed in each activity, extracting greater richness while simultaneously enhancing your attentional skills. You're not multitasking; you're unitasking. Rather than constantly stacking inputs, you're giving your full attention to a single stream of embodied awareness, noticing the felt sensations, physical feedback loops, and internal experiences unfolding in each moment. Over time, this mindful engagement with the mundane steadily builds your capacity for sustained focus and presence amidst any activity or environment. You're exercising the cognitive muscles and creating the neural pathways required for peak performance during your biggest priorities and creative challenges.

Instead of draining mental resources by rapidly shifting between disparate contexts and inputs, you're allowing integrated recharging and centering to occur. You're giving your executive functioning and intuitive mind the equal opportunity to process experiences so they can optimally synthesize during periods of deeper work. In this way, making routine behaviors more mindful isn't another draining multitasking; it's the antidote to our cultural addictions to busyness and partial distraction. Think of it as a recovery of sorts. It's a paradoxical recalibration back to the fundamentals of how our minds were designed to operate optimally.

Navigating the Currents of Modern Life: Quick Techniques for Presence, Stress Reduction, and Seamless Meditation

By harnessing the power of focused attention and intentional awareness, you can transform the seemingly ordinary into portals for profound stress reduction, personal growth, and a deeper connection to the world around you.

By integrating mindful practices into your daily rituals, you cultivate an oasis of tranquility amidst the currents of modern life. This enables you to tackle even the most hectic schedules with grace, clarity, and a profound sense of inner peace.

Mindful Sustenance: Eating With Presence

The act of nourishing your body is one of the most fundamental human experiences, yet it is often reduced to a mindless ritual punctuated by hurried bites and distracted consumption. Reclaiming the sacred act of eating through mindfulness can enhance your appreciation for the food you consume and cultivate a profound sense of presence and stress relief.

- **Savor the senses:** Before taking the first bite, pause and fully engage your senses. Look at the colors, textures, and aromas of your meal, savoring the anticipation of taste. As you eat, consciously go through every experience: the flavors, textures, and sensations, resisting the urge to rush.

- **Appreciate the journey:** Reflect on the intricate journey your food has undertaken, from the soil, sun, and water that nurtured its growth to the hands that harvested and prepared it. This fosters a sense of gratitude and interconnectedness with the natural world.

- **Mindful chewing:** By simply slowing down and chewing each bite thoroughly, you aid digestion and create a meditative rhythm that anchors you in the present moment, allowing stress and worries to dissipate.

The Sacred Stroll: Walking With Intention

The simple act of walking can become a mindless transit from one point to another. But, by infusing this routine activity with intention and awareness, you can transform it into a moving meditation, cultivating presence and reducing stress with every step.

- **Breath awareness:** As you begin your walk, bring your attention to your breath, noting the rise and fall of your abdomen or the sensation of air passing through your nostrils. Synchronize your steps with your inhales and exhales to create a rhythmic cadence.

- **Sensory immersion:** Fully engage all your senses, including the sights, sounds, smells, and tactile sensations of your surroundings. Notice the play of light and shadow, the texture of the ground beneath your feet, and the scents carried on the breeze to anchor you in the present moment.

- **Mantra or affirmation:** Choose a simple phrase or affirmation that resonates with you, and silently repeat it with each step, allowing it to infuse your stride with intention and focus.

The Sound of Stillness: Listening With Mindful Presence

The art of truly listening (to the sounds around us, to the voices of loved ones, and even to the whispers of our own thoughts) can become a forgotten skill. By cultivating mindful listening, you can reduce stress, enhance your communication, and deepen your connection to the present moment.

- **Environmental soundscapes:** Periodically, pause and tune into the symphony of sounds surrounding you: the hum of traffic, the rustle of leaves, the distant laughter of children at play. Allow yourself to fully immerse in this auditory experience, resisting the urge to label or judge the sounds but simply experiencing them as they arise and dissipate.

- **Active listening:** In conversations, resist the temptation to formulate your response while the other person is speaking. Give them your undivided attention, focusing not just on their words but on the tone, inflection, and body language that accompanies them. This cultivates empathy and understanding and reduces the stress of miscommunication. Another great aspect is the fact that you will make the other person feel heard and valued.

- **Inner dialogue:** Just as you can mindfully listen to external sounds, you can also turn your attention inward and observe the constant stream of thoughts, emotions, and internal narratives that shape your experience. By simply noticing these mental phenomena with a non-judgmental stance, you create space for clarity and reduce the grip of stress-inducing rumination.

Seamless Integration: Establishing Consistent Meditation Habits

By seamlessly integrating meditation into your daily routines, you can cultivate a consistent practice that becomes a natural and effortless aspect of your life, enabling you to maintain a state of mindful presence and tranquility.

- **Commuting contemplation:** Whether driving, taking public transportation, or even walking to your destination, the time spent commuting can be transformed into a moving meditation. Engage in breath awareness and body scans, or repeat a mantra or affirmation to anchor your attention in the present moment.

- **Waiting room wisdom:** Rather than succumbing to the restlessness and impatience of waiting (whether in line at the grocery store, at the doctor's office, or anywhere else), use these pockets of time as opportunities for mindfulness. Tune into your breath, cultivate gratitude, or practice loving-kindness toward yourself and those around you.

- **Household mindfulness:** Infuse mundane household tasks, such as washing dishes, folding laundry, or even brushing your teeth, with a sense of presence and awareness. Rather than allowing your mind to wander, focus your attention fully on the sensory experience of the task at hand, savoring each moment.

- **Nature's embrace:** Whenever possible, step outside and immerse yourself in the natural world, even if just for a few moments. Allow the sights, sounds, and scents of nature to ground you in the present, fostering a sense of awe and connection with the world beyond the confines of your daily routine.

Techniques for Seamless Meditation Integration

- Set reminders or alarms to prompt mindful pauses throughout the day.

- Leverage existing routines, such as brushing your teeth or waiting for the kettle to boil, as opportunities for meditation.

- Keep it simple; even a few conscious breaths can shift your state of being.

- Experiment with different techniques to find what resonates best with you.

- Be patient and gentle with yourself; no judgment allowed!

- Remember: Consistency is key!

- Seek out guided meditations or apps for added structure and support.

What to Avoid

- Don't multitask during meditation, as it negates the benefits of present-moment awareness.

- Avoid judging or resisting thoughts and emotions that arise; simply observe them with compassionate acceptance.

- Don't expect immediate results; personal growth and stress reduction are cultivated through consistent practice over time.

- Try not to cling to specific techniques or beliefs; meditation is a means of exploration, not dogma.

Each intentional pause, each conscious breath, becomes a powerful anchor, grounding you in the present moment and reminding you of the profound beauty and richness that resides within the seemingly ordinary. In this way, you cultivate a profound appreciation for the present moment, realizing that life is, in actuality, extraordinary.

While these ancient practices provide the grounding foundation, modern technology offers new ways to elevate and augment your meditation journey. From immersive audio environments to real-time brainwave tracking, innovative tools are enhancing our mindfulness. Let's explore how to harmonize the timeless wisdom of contemplative traditions with cutting-edge innovations.

Chapter 12:

Improving Meditation With Technology

Technology is a useful servant but a dangerous master. –Christian Lous Lange

I once spent a solid week in total silence at a Zen Buddhist monastery. There was no talking, reading, or digital leashes. Aside from ritualized meal times and the intermittent ringing of ambient setting awakening bells, my senses were fully immersed in profoundly ordinary present moments.

Each breath was kissed by the aroma of smoldering incense and fresh tatami mats. Even the simple acts of properly holding a bowl of rice or meticulously folding my robes unveiled new dimensions of intimacy with tactile aliveness. Sounds like a veritable "awakened one's" dream of an experience, right? No apps, no guides, no self-dopamine pellets. Just nowness. Well... at least until that first din of the morning when my iPhone alarm rudely shattered the pristine stillness, jolting me back into unmindful doing mode for the dreaded morning commute. One Uber ride, two train changes, and a shuttle bus later, I found myself planted amidst that oh-so-glamorously gritty NYC rush hour hustle.

As the familiar swell of overstimulated anxiety rose alongside the beeping horns and barked profanities, I instinctively summoned the only tool I had at my disposal—the simple acknowledgment of my breath. In through the nose, out through the mouth. One inhalation at a time.

The fidgety guy loudly slurping a McLatté beside me morphed from an isolated annoyance into an ambient aspect. Even the migraine-inducing fluorescent hum overhead somehow integrated into the transient orchestra. By the time I stepped off that final subway car, I felt like a rainforest creature freshly born. Here I was, mere moments after frenetically thrusting myself through the metropolitan membrane, feeling as anchored and appreciative as when upholding those meticulously choreographed Zen routines. In that instant, something transcended. I had transformed the thoroughly mundane into something entirely profound with nothing more than a simple rewiring of perception.

Why am I sharing this admittedly contrived tale of mystical urban attainment? Aside from obviously indulging in some quintessentially privileged cosmopolitan navel-gazing, it reveals an empowering truth about the nature of presence and our potential relationship to it.

Merging of Ancient and New Age

Meditation's heart lies in an ancient tradition dating back thousands of years. The purposeful cultivation of present-moment awareness has long been revered from Buddhist monasteries to Hindu ashrams.

These timeless practices were passed down from mentor to student, existing in a spiritual world seemingly untouched by the rapid march of technological progress. But fast-forward to our hyper-connected 21st-century lives, and an intriguing crossroads has emerged. Might the seamless union of meditation's contemplative roots with cutting-edge innovations enhance our ability to dwell in mindfulness? Or does excessive reliance on digital tools simply become another distraction undermining presence?

The answers, like many truths, lie somewhere between the extremes. Technology's role in evolving meditation depends largely on our skill and intention as users. Used responsibly, these new tools can democratize ancient practices. But left unchecked, they risk corrupting the authenticity at the heart of the path.

Let's get a better understanding of the era of the meditation app:

- **Statistics speak volumes about shifting demographics (Singh, 2024):**
    - Searches for yoga and meditation apps rose 65% year-over-year from 2019 to 2020.
    - The top 10 meditation apps had 52 million downloads in 2019.
    - The meditation app market revenue is projected to reach $6.7 billion by 2026.
    - Over 2,500 new meditation mobile apps were launched between 2015-2020.
    - The top 10 meditation apps generated $195 million in revenue.
    - North America is the top market, with a projected 5% CAGR by 2032.
    - The number of meditators in the United States has tripled since 2012.
    - The U.S. meditation market is valued at $2.08 billion in 2022.
    - Meditation apps are the third most purchased health app category in the U.S.
    - iOS is preferred over Android for meditation apps.
    - Android meditation apps forecast $74 million in revenue by 2029.
    - 53% of U.S. seniors meditate at least weekly.

- Child meditation rates surged 800% since 2012.
- 16% of women meditate regularly vs. 12% of men.
- Popular features include audio/video playback and personalization.
- The VR meditation market could reach $3.9 billion by 2023.

- **Features powering these tools' booming popularity include:**
  - From pocket-sized reminders to on-the-go practices, these tools are convenient and accessible.
  - Guided instruction is available for varying expertise levels.
  - Ever-expanding content libraries personalize experiences.
  - Community-building and shared insights offer value.
  - Innovations are enhanced by evolving technologies like AI, VR, biometrics, and more.

- **Significant criticisms of app-based meditation exist:**
  - There is monetization of mindfulness through paid subscriptions and consumption metrics.
  - "McDonaldization" reduces nuanced traditions to overly simplistic formulas.
  - Algorithms are prioritized over individualized, human-led instruction.

- Distractibility is exacerbated by introducing yet another digital addiction.

Essentially, meditation apps reflect a double-edged sword capable of expanding access while potentially diluting authenticity. Much depends on the user's motivations and level of commitment.

How Tech Tools Can Enhance the Journey

When leveraged skillfully, technology undoubtedly augments the meditation experience in powerful ways:

- **Convenience and consistency:** The ability to quickly reference guides, timers, and teachings wherever you go greatly aids the development of a regular sitting habit.

- **Gateway to understanding:** For those new to meditation, apps and videos gently demystify and democratize what were once seen as esoteric practices only available through monasteries and ashrams. Interactive content can teach fundamentals like breathwork or mantras in highly accessible, relatable formats.

- **Personalized customization:** With an ever-growing library of meditations targeting varied goals, traditions, and experience levels, technology enables you to precisely calibrate your practice. From sleep-optimized sessions to athletic performance visualizations, the options match any interest.

- **Measurable data and motivation:** Talk about a win-win! Devices capable of tracking your biological feedback, such as brainwave patterns, heart rates, and muscle tension, give tangible reinforcement that you're making progress. This boosts the incentive to continue by revealing meditation's physiological impacts.

- **Online community support:** While reduced social risk allows beginners to comfortably explore meditation at their own pace, the potential for bonding with like-minded people is an option. This sense of togetherness and shared insights foster accountability and encouragement.

How Tech Can Enable Distraction

However, tread carefully to prevent these tools from becoming impediments:

- **Digital disruption and inability to unplug:** By their very nature, smartphones, notifications, and apps have the potential to fragment our attention and presence rather than centering it. Just think about endless hours of mindless scrolling, right? For the meditation practitioner, excessive reliance on electronics can ironically feed the very distractions they're trying to transcend.

- **The danger of overstimulation:** From endless audio and video content libraries to virtual reality odysseys, the human mind can easily become overstimulated by an overwhelming flood of stimuli. At a certain point, the sheer abundance of options creates a scattered focus, strongly contradicting stillness. Does analysis paralysis ring any bells?

- **The monetization of mindfulness:** When is it not all about the money, honey? With multi-billion dollar investments pouring into the meditation app space, skeptics warn of the purity and authenticity of these teachings being sacrificed at the altar of mass commercialization. Is "awareness for profit" simply an oxymoron?

- **Disconnection from human teachers:** While democratized learning opens doors, there's an intimacy lost when wisdom gets overly technologized.

- **Fueling addictive digital habits:** Even with the best intentions, continually reaching for an app or digital device out of habit can become a mindless compulsion defeating meditation's greater purpose. We simply swap one form of distractibility for another.

The most balanced approach acknowledges both the extraordinary potential and inherent limitations of fusing technology with meditation. It's all about balance.

Perhaps the greatest truths regarding technology's role in meditation come from the Buddha's timeless wisdom of taking the "middle way"—avoiding the extremes of blind rejection or overzealous attachment.

These digital tools are double-edged swords, capable of uplifting or undermining your journey depending on how you relate to them. Like fair-weather friends, they can inspire and encourage your highest self while seducing you into distraction if not kept in a healthy perspective. Rather than falling victim to reactivity, consciously remember that no technology can serve as a replacement for the inner work required. Apps can introduce methods, and data can reveal patterns, but you alone must do the labor of quieting the fluctuations of the mind through embodied presence. At their best, these innovations open doors into timeless wisdom long reserved for those with resources to study under masters.

Used responsibly, digital tools provide entry points for beginners while allowing seasoned practitioners to deepen their understanding through personalization. At their worst, excessive reliance on technology repackages authenticity into commodities governed by bottom lines rather than dharma (generally refers to the underlying order in nature and life and an individual's duties and moral responsibilities). Where we once created sacred spaces for contemplation, we risk corroding meaning into mere transactions for profit. Perhaps the healthiest integration balances the yin and yang of the old with the new, melding the rigor of ancient lineages with the empowerment of democratized access and choice. It's a path of recognizing innovation as a tool enhancing your personal journey without allowing it to become the destination.

When you root your relationship with technology in an ethical framework guided by compassion, humility, and restraint, you open to the highest expression of these powerful capabilities. Apps and digital aids should remain precisely that: aids, not replacements. Only you can do the sacred inner work to which no shortcut exists.

Blending Tradition With Innovation

For centuries, the path of meditation remained relatively untouched by humanity's scientific and technological revolutions. Practices like breath awareness, mantra repetition, and loving-kindness visualization were preserved through an unbroken lineage of oral tradition and sacred texts.

Today, we find these timeless teachings undergoing an intriguing metamorphosis. An era of unprecedented innovation sparking a modern meditation renaissance. From AI-powered apps to immersive virtual reality, meditators now interface with an arsenal of tech capable of dramatically enhancing our inner work. Yes, this convergence of ancient and new obviously raises both enthusiastic possibilities as well as valid concerns. The key lies in our relationship with these technologies, wrangling them as supportive allies rather than becoming enslaved by their potential distractions.

Meditating Through the Digital Lens

Using technologies designed for productivity and entertainment to further one's meditation practice may seem paradoxical at first glance.

Yet the rapid rise of this space reveals an undeniable demand from modern seekers. What's behind all these striking numbers and stats?

An incredible array of digitally augmented features and modalities, each creatively enhancing elements of traditional practice. So, what's in it for you?

- **Immersive 360° VR environments:** Using apps like Tripp or Nature Trek VR, meditators can transport themselves into ultra-realistic 3D landscapes scientifically optimized for present-moment engagement, from visually stunning beaches to psychedelic spirit realms, artificial yet highly experiential, transcending the confines of the physical.

- **Biofeedback and physiological tracking:** Wearable biosensors combined with smartphone integration allow many modern apps like Core to deliver real-time data on factors like heart rate variability, respiration, and brainwave states. This quantifiable feedback is a great motivator.

- **Artificial intelligence personalization:** By analyzing factors like personality types, brainwave signatures, and physiological patterns, innovative AI systems like Mind can custom-tailor entire meditation programs to each individual's unique needs and tendencies.

- **Breathwork and visualization technology:** Apps like Prana Breath and Journey Meditation use interactive graphics and soothing audio to guide focused breathwork, mantra concentration, and detailed visualization exercises proven to harmonize mind-body awareness.

- **Gamified motivation and social elements:** Following the model of fitness apps, programs like Meditation.live include features like in-app trophies, badges, and synchronized practice sessions to increase accountability and satisfaction.

- **Expansive multimedia content libraries**: With in-app subscription models, many popular platforms provide an endless array of guided meditations, sleep stories, music, and inspirational talks from renowned experts across all major practice traditions.

These rapidly evolving technologies empower meditators with enhanced personalization, immersion, motivation, and real-time physiological feedback compared to conventional practice. But be wary and keep a realistic mind. All transformative new frontiers also present significant risks and limitations if not counterbalanced by wisdom and discipline.

As the Buddhists remind us, our highest spiritual priorities must involve detaching from compulsive cravings and transcending conceptual fixations. Enlightenment cannot be simulated through algorithms; remember that. At its core, meditation represents a comprehensive path of awakening by radically reorienting our relationship to experience itself. Apps and devices, regardless of sophistication, remain external tools capable of cultivating initial conditions yet powerless to fully manifest that internal shift in consciousness.

Integrating Technology and Tradition

Skillful and balanced integration of the ancient with the contemporary opens up an empowering middle way. If you approach technology with pragmatic clarity about all the intended supportive roles and inherent limitations, it becomes a powerful ally turbo-charging the development of your lived experience.

Let's look at some thoughtful ways to harmonize tradition and technology:

- **Establishing a foundational understanding:** You need to understand what you're working with. Before augmenting meditation with any digital tools, first develop a baseline familiarity with traditional frameworks, lineages, and core techniques. You can opt for in-person guidance with an experienced teacher. Only with this foundation can technologies' appropriate role emerge.

- **Utilizing technology as an initial entry point:** For beginners, guided apps and introductory content offer an on-ramp into learning fundamentals like breathwork, body scans, and concentration practices. This will help reduce initial barriers while establishing basic skills.

- **Supporting discipline through reminders and accountability:** Simple tech features like scheduled notifications, synced practice groups, and gamified motivation help establish and maintain a consistent habit.

- **Enhancing personalization and real-time feedback:** Innovative personalization through AI and wearable biometric tracking allows you to thoughtfully optimize your practice based on ever-refining data about physiological states and patterns. Pretty cool!

- **Complementing physical practice with virtual tools:** While in-person sits and time in nature remain first prize, guided visualizations, breathwork animations, and ultra-immersive VR environments provide rich supplemental resources for deepening focus and relaxation.

- **Limiting overuse of apps and tracking:** Establish reasonable parameters for app integration to avoid obsessive quantification or content bingeing.

- **Emphasizing ethics and healthy relationships with tech:** A good rule of thumb is to always investigate the integrity and motivations of digital platforms. Prioritizing mission-driven services over those solely profit-focused promotes the right intentions and non-attachment.

You can investigate and

- research the founders and leadership.
- evaluate the mission statement.
- assess privacy and data policies.
- review user feedback and testimonials.
- investigate funding sources.
- analyze the business model.
- check for community and customer support.
- look for industry recognition and awards.
- verify partnerships and collaborations.
- test the platform yourself.

Through this middle-way approach, you honor tradition while also opening yourself to the profound enhancements modern technology provides.

At their best, these innovative technologies represent marvels of democratizing access, customization, and scientific understanding to reveal our most sublime human potential. At their worst, they simply reinforce the compulsive avoidance and addiction patterns endemic to the human condition.

App Suggestions

It's all about merging the ancient with the ultra-modern! Mixing old-school meditation with new-age tech was practically made for us hustlers! The choice resides firmly within you. You alone decide whether to wield these powerful tools with discipline and clarity of intention or succumb to their endless allures of cognitive candy.

For now, here is a list of some meditation apps worth looking into:

- **VR meditation apps**
    - Tripp
    - Nature Treks VR
- **AI-powered meditation apps**
    - Headspace
    - Calm
    - Wysa
    - Aura
    - Ten Percent Happier
    - Moodfit
    - Unmind
- **Biofeedback and physiological tracking**
    - Core Meditation
    - Muse
    - HeartMath
- **Breathwork and visualization technology**
    - Prana Breath
    - Journey Meditation

- Breathe2Relax

- **Gamified motivation and social elements**
  - Meditation.live
  - Insight Timer
  - Simple Habit

- **General meditation apps**
  - Breethe
  - Sattva
  - Smiling Mind
  - The Mindfulness App
  - Buddhify
  - Omvana
  - Insight Timer

- **Specialized meditation content**
  - Calm (for sleep stories and relaxing music)
  - Insight Timer (for a large library of guided meditations)
  - 10% Happier (for mindfulness education)

- **Workplace and corporate-focused**
  - Unmind
  - Headspace for Work

- Calm for Business

- **Therapy and mental health integration**

    - Wysa (with therapeutic techniques)

    - Happify

    - Sanvello

These are just a couple of examples to get you started. There's a whole wide web out there to explore!

On that transcendental note, a graceful mind-bridge into our next chapter: We've now surveyed meditation's convergence with the digital world. Let's pivot toward the rigorously structured and empirically validated—the cutting-edge science illuminating this ancient awareness's myriad benefits. "Scientifically Sound Practices" will demystify many misconceptions while revealing how even discretely micro-dosing mindfulness ignites profound ripples throughout your existence. So, settle in!

Chapter 13:

Scientifically Sound Practices

Between stimulus and response, there is a space. In that space is our power to choose our response. In our response lies our growth and our freedom. –Victor Frankl

You know that friend who's always subtweeting philosophical musings after their latest spirit quest? Or that one co-worker who can't stop evangelizing about some random biohacking protocol they gunned from a suspect Gaia Q-Anon influencer?

When it comes to unpacking the real-world pragmatism behind meditation and mindfulness, I low-key play the role of a mystical party-pooper. Don't get me wrong; I've certainly drunk more than my fair share of metaphysical Kool-Aid after stumbling west from the halls of elite institutional neurotoxicity in search of liberation. But at this point, I've put in enough years and data points hopping between contemplative urban ashrams, somatic nervous system rewiring labs, and IEEE (IEEE plays a critical role in the dissemination of knowledge and the setting of technological standards that ensure interoperability and quality) panels on augmented intelligence to develop a finely calibrated knowledge base for cutting through the woo-woo with some science-respecting nuance. Look, I'm all for the brain-boosting benefits and neurocircuit rewiring that a good mindfulness routine can bring. I've been following the neuroimaging studies and clinical research that show how meditation helps with anxiety, ADHD, and insomnia for years. I get it—just a few minutes of mindfulness each day can significantly improve focus, emotional control, and a sense of inner peace.

But we have to keep it real: No matter how much you hear about meditation's immediate benefits, it's essential to remember that simply practicing mindfulness or sensory awareness won't completely change your basic human instincts. What meditation does offer are optimized mental states of being present in your body. With consistent practice, it helps reshape your habits of disconnecting and avoiding challenges, which often keep you from reaching your full potential.

But I'm getting ahead of myself here.

For this chapter, let's start by unpacking some key studies that shine scientific luminance on the whole "I don't have time to meditate because I have a busy life" misconception. Meditation is not about achieving a constant state of perfect calm but about gradually improving your ability to be fully present and aware of whatever you do. It's about taking regular pauses, which eventually culminates in a better quality of life.

The Science of Everyday Meditation

Busy humans, assemble! While movies showcasing the spiritual journeys of celebrities like Brad Pitt might be entertaining, we must look beyond the hype and focus on the real, measurable benefits that meditation and mindfulness can offer regular folks like us in our busy everyday lives.

You don't have to slather yourself in ghee, broadcast OM frequencies on a perpetual loop, or, worst of all, cancel your Netflix subscription indefinitely. It's just a pragmatic recalibration of perception catalyzed by being mindful and fully present in our bodies.

Let's explore some highlights from the cutting edge of modern mind science. All you need is an open, curious mind willing to look beyond the buzzwords of "disruptive innovation" and embrace practical, proven techniques for "reaching the peak of mindful awareness."

The following studies provide some empirical support for the general concepts mentioned throughout these pages about brief meditation/mindfulness practices helping to reduce physiological/psychological stress and improve mood.

Psychological Benefits

- A study published in *Psychoneuroendocrinology* found that short meditation sessions can significantly reduce stress levels. Participants who meditated for 10 minutes showed decreased cortisol levels (Tang et al., 2007).

- Another study demonstrated that even brief mindfulness exercises can lower perceived stress in college students during exam periods, indicating the potential for a quick meditation to alleviate acute stress (Bergen-Cico et al., 2013).

- A pilot study published in the *Journal of Internal General Medicine* found that a four-week mindfulness program reduced physiological stress (heart rate, blood pressure) in healthcare professionals (Plews-Ogan et al., 2005).

- In *Psychoneuroendocrinology*, it showed that a three-day mindfulness meditation training helped reduce stress and improve mood in response to a social evaluative stress task in participants with high-stress occupations and lifestyles (Creswell et al., 2014).

Cognitive Benefits

- A study in *Psychological Science* revealed that a mere eight-week mindfulness training course could enhance cognitive performance and improve working memory capacity and attention (Jha et al., 2010).

- The *Journal of Neuroscience* published findings that four days of meditation training can improve performance on the working memory and cognitive control aspects of the n-back task, a cognitive exercise used to measure and evaluate a person's working memory and cognitive control capabilities (Zeidan et al., 2010).

- Research in *Psychological Science* found that a two-week mindfulness training program can improve attentional control and reduce mind wandering (Morrison et al., 2014).

- Research from *Psychological Science* found that a 15-minute mindfulness induction can improve insight, problem-solving, and decision-making performance (Ostafin & Kassman, 2012).

- Another study published in *Psychological Science* demonstrated that a brief mindfulness meditation training can reduce negative affect and increase cognitive flexibility in decision-making, and 8 minutes of mindful breathing reduces behavioral indicators of mind wandering (Mrazek et al., 2013).

- A study in *Psychological Science* found that mindfulness practice reduces sunk-cost bias in decision-making (Hafenbrack et al., 2014).

- Research in the *Journal of Applied Psychology* indicated that mindfulness practice positively relates to ethical decision-making through increased moral attentiveness (Ruedy & Schweitzer, 2010).

Physical Benefits

- A study published in *Current Hypertension Reports* showed that device-guided slow breathing can reduce blood pressure in hypertensive patients (Brook et al., 2013).

- Research published in the *Journal of Human Hypertension* confirmed that an eight-week mindfulness program can help significantly reduce blood pressure (Hughes et al., 2013).

- Research conducted by researchers by the NIH-funded Institute of Natural Medicine and Prevention at Maharishi University of Management and the University of Kentucky College of Medicine indicated that transcendental meditation is an effective non-pharmacologic intervention for managing hypertension compared to other stress reduction programs.

- The *Journal of Neuroscience* reported that brief mindfulness meditation training can reduce pain perception and brain response to pain (Zeidan et al., 2011).

- Another study in the *Journal of Neuroscience* found that brief mindfulness meditation training alters brain activity in regions associated with pain processing (Zeidan et al., 2015).

- Research in *JAMA Internal Medicine* demonstrated that mindfulness meditation programs may significantly reduce chronic lower back pain and improve functional limitations (Cherkin et al., 2016).

- A study in *Pain* found that brief mindfulness training can reduce pain perception and brain response to pain stimuli (Zeidan et al., 2010).

Practical Applications for Busy Lives

- Research in the *Journal of Occupational Health Psychology* highlighted that workplace mindfulness training can enhance employee well-being and job performance (Good et al., 2016).

- A study in the *Journal of Occupational and Organizational Psychology* found that a workplace mindfulness intervention reduced burnout and improved well-being (Shonin et al. 2014).

- This study published in the journal *Psychological Research* in 2022 found that induced state mindfulness reduced the sunk-cost bias in a repeated decision-making task, improving employee well-being and organizational performance (Hafenbrack et al., 2013).

- A study in *Mindfulness* indicated that a workplace mindfulness program improved job satisfaction, emotional exhaustion, and personal accomplishment (Hülsheger et al., 2013).

- The *Journal of Experimental Psychology: Applied* published findings that a brief mindfulness induction reduced mind-wandering and improved performance on the GRE for students and improved reading comprehension scores via improved working memory capacity (Mrazek et al., 2013).

- A study in *Mindfulness* found that a brief mindfulness curriculum helped students improve cognitive control and reduce stress and anxiety, leading to improved emotion regulation and well-being (Broderick & Metz, 2009).

- Research in the *Journal of Child and Family Studies* indicated that a mindfulness education program improved student psychosocial outcomes and sleep quality (Felver et al., 2016).

Techniques for Quick Meditation Sessions

- A study in *Biological Psychology* found that brief breath awareness exercises can reduce negative subjective and physiological consequences of stress (Arch & Craske, 2006).

- Research published in *Behaviour Research and Therapy* showed that a brief breathing meditation can reduce negative mood and increase present-moment awareness (Erisman & Roemer, 2010).

- A study in *Psychophysiology* reported that focused breathing exercises can regulate autonomic nervous system activity (Burg et al., 2012).

- Research in *Mindfulness* indicated that brief breath awareness training can improve emotion regulation ability (Arch & Craske, 2006).

- The *Journal of Behavioral Medicine* reported that a brief body scan meditation may have a significant reduction in ratings for pain-related distress and for pain interfering with social relations (Ussher et al., 2012).

- Research in *JAMA Internal Medicine* demonstrated that mindfulness meditation, including body scans, can improve sleep quality (Black et al., 2015).

- A study published by *The American Psychological Association* indicated that body scan meditation can reduce emotional reactivity (Sauer & Baer, 2010).

- Research in the *International Journal of Environmental Research and Public Health* indicated that mindful walking combined with forest therapy can improve psychological well-being (Kim et al., 2020).

- A study in *Preventative Medicine Reports* demonstrated that mindful walking can improve cognitive function and reduce perceived stress (Yang et al., 2021).

Long-Term Benefits of Regular Quick Meditation

- The *Journal of Consulting and Clinical Psychology* published findings that mindfulness-based cognitive therapy can help prevent depressive relapses (Teasdale et al., 2000). Another study published in the same journal found that a mindfulness-based relapse prevention program reduced the risk of depressive relapse over as little as a one-year period (Kuyken et al., 2008). This is rather significant for people struggling with depression.

- Research published in *Annals of Behavioral Medicine* demonstrated that mindfulness training can lead to sustained decreases in depression, anxiety, and stress over three years (Jain et al., 2007).

- Research in *Psychosomatic Medicine* indicated that mindfulness training can increase cognitive resilience to stress (Creswell et al., 2007).

- The *Journal of Clinical Psychology* found that mindfulness training helped improve resilience, reduce perceived stress, and improve overall well-being and quality of life (Nyklíček & Kuijpers, 2008).

- A study published in *APA PsycNet* reported that mindfulness-based therapy can enhance psychological resilience in individuals with PTSD (Vujanovic et al., 2013).

- Another study also published in *APA PsycNet* demonstrated that mindfulness training enhances resilience by facilitating adaptive coping (Weinstein et al., 2009).

There's not just one study backing up the benefits; this is merely the tip of the iceberg. Give it a whirl, and you'll unlock a treasure trove of benefits firsthand!

As the mountain of peer-reviewed data continues growing, one clear truth emerges: You don't need to embody a spiritual caricature or rigidly conform to any particular dogma or lineage. Mindfulness is a universally pragmatic toolkit for optimizing your whole being to meet the complex demands of our time. Whatever your background or daily routine, research shows you can always find a way to hit "pause" on the incessant narrative loops and habituated reactivity to recalibrate.

Mindfulness isn't another checkbox task to frantically pursue and acquire; it's a playful reconnection with the essence of what it means to live consciously.

Whether struggling through apparent stressors or simply seeking greater vitality, aspects of mindfulness like breath awareness, body scanning, mantra repetition, and intentional pausing will serve to defrag your overcrowded consciousness. The dividends of heightening your relationship with embodied presence create positive feedback loops that reverberate into every aspect of life.

Simply being here fully catalyzes expansive transformation. Hopefully, these highlights provide ample reassurance that you don't need another torpedo of insecurity aimed at your sense of self-worth.

Say What?

You've learned about the science-backed benefits. You've seen mindfulness's profound impact on reducing stress, enhancing cognition, improving physical health, and bolstering resilience. But have you truly allowed these revelations to sink in?

Imagine a life where your full potential is finally unleashed. A life of unshakable calm amid the storms of stress and chaos. A life where your mind operates with surgical precision—creative insights are flowing, tough decisions are made with clarity, and goals are achieved through heightened focus and productivity. This isn't a pipe dream. This is the power you gain by embracing daily mindfulness. To top it all off, this ultimate personal and professional upgrade requires only 10–15 minutes per day from you. Just a few stray moments of intention and presence are all it takes to access mindfulness' extraordinary effects. An investment of 1% of your day can return exponential dividends across the other 99%! It's like a software update for your mind and mood.

The possibilities revealed by the latest mindfulness research are limited only by our own resistance. Why continue sleepwalking through life on autopilot when 10 minutes of conscious presence can unlock your highest human potential? This is an invitation to step into your power in every arena of life. No longer must mindfulness be shrouded in New Age mystery. This is a rigorously studied, scientifically validated construct for awakening the mind, body, and spirit, all while requiring only a few purposefully present moments from you each day. This transformative power is available to you right now.

Conclusion

Gratitude is not just a word; it's an attitude that changes everything. –Shubham Shukla

As we bid a fond farewell to our journey through *Minute Meditations for the Real World,* it's time to pause and absorb the main event: the profound yet practical power of mindfulness.

In our relentless pursuit of success and outpacing that polka-dotted "productivity unicorn," we often find ourselves caught in a whirlwind of demands and distractions. Yet, the key to mastering time lies not in acquiring more tools and hacks but in embracing the simplicity of present-moment awareness.

This book has illustrated the myriad benefits of mindfulness—from anxiety relief and enhanced focus to improved emotional regulation and heightened productivity. The remarkable adaptability of these ancient practices to our contemporary context stands out as a testament to their enduring value. *Minute Meditations for the Real World* is more than a guide; it's an invitation to transform your life one mindful moment at a time.

The sublime beauty of mindfulness lies in its ingenious simplicity—simply stealing a few conscious breaths, gentle body scan sessions, or mindful stretches can transport you into momentary nirvana amid the daily storms. This book's promise is to integrate ancient wisdom with modern practicality to help you achieve lasting peace, health, productivity, and efficiency.

These practices anchor you to the present, preventing you from being swept away by anxiety and overwhelm. Mindfulness is not just a respite from stress; it is a powerful catalyst for personal growth and excellence in all facets of life.

By training your mind to embrace the present with radical acceptance, you develop the cognitive flexibility to navigate challenges with resilience, adaptability, and creativity. The act of mindful presence becomes a wellspring of insight, innovation, and emotional intelligence—invaluable assets in our ever-evolving world.

The scientific evidence is clear: mindfulness enhances focus, reduces stress, improves sleep, and bolsters resilience. More importantly, it transforms the quality of your daily life, one moment at a time. Embrace mindfulness not as a passing fad but as a lifelong companion. Integrate these practices into your daily routine, from your commute to your workday, your downtime, and even your most mundane chores.

In the end, time is your most precious commodity. Mindfulness empowers you to savor each moment, extract the essence of experience, and approach every endeavor with clarity and focus. This is the true power of *Minute Meditations for the Real World*—to help you live life to its fullest potential, one breath at a time, one moment at a time.

With these mindful upgrades installed, you now possess the mental fortitude to gracefully navigate life's plot twists and challenges. Relish them, expand on them, share them far and wide—start a mindful epidemic that reshapes the entire human collective into a wiser, kinder, more self-actualized existence that we can all enjoy.

May each inhalation be savored, every sight absorbed in high-definition, and all the magic potentials of pure presence actualized beyond your wildest daydreams.

Your feedback is invaluable—please consider leaving an honest review to help others discover the benefits of *Minute Meditations for the Real World*.

Existence awaits!

Scan QR code to LEAVE A REVIEW

If You Liked This Book, You Might Also Like...

Inner Child Recovery Workbook
Healing Your Inner Child from Childhood Trauma, Abandonment, and Abuse to Find Peace and Happiness

SCAN ME!

Self-Love Workbook for Men
Discover Your Worth, Defeat Fear and Doubt, and Build Unshakable Confidence

SCAN ME!

References

A step-by-step guide to finding your meditation posture. (2023, June 25). Mindful Society Global Institute. https://www.mindfulinstitute.org/blog/article-a-step-by-step-guide-to-finding-your-meditation-posture

Ahlschlager, J. (2020, August 6). *Engage in the 5 pillars of resilience during tough times.* Vital Work Life. https://insights.vitalworklife.com/engage-in-the-5-pillars-of-resilience-during-tough-times

Akita, L. G. (n.d.). *Wellness quotes.* Goodreads. https://www.goodreads.com/quotes/tag/wellness

Amano, T., & Toichi, M. (2016). The role of alternating bilateral stimulation in establishing positive cognition in EMDR therapy: A multi-channel near-infrared spectroscopy study. *PLoS ONE, 11*(10). https://doi.org/10.1371/journal.pone.0162735

Anālayo, B. (n.d.). *External mindfulness.* Insight Meditation Society. https://www.dharma.org/external-mindfulness/

Arch, J. J., & Craske, M. G. (2006). Mechanisms of mindfulness: Emotion regulation following a focused breathing induction. *Behaviour Research and Therapy, 44*(12), 1849–1858. https://doi.org/10.1016/j.brat.2005.12.007

Babauta, L. (n.d.). *Meditation for beginners: 20 Practical tips for understanding the mind.* Zen Habits. https://zenhabits.net/meditation-guide/

Baer, M. B. (2023, March 15). *Empathy and self-awareness.* Psychology Today.

https://www.psychologytoday.com/intl/blog/empathy-and-relationships/202303/empathy-and-self-awareness

Benton, L. (2019, October 16). *How to embed mindfulness in the workplace?* Liberty Mind. https://libertymind.co.uk/how-to-embed-mindfulness-in-the-workplace/

Bergen-Cico, D., Possemato, K., & Cheon, S. (2013). Examining the efficacy of a brief mindfulness-based stress reduction (brief MBSR) program on psychological health. *Journal of American College Health*, *61*(6), 348–360. https://doi.org/10.1080/07448481.2013.813853

Black, D. S., O'Reilly, G. A., Olmstead, R., Breen, E. C., & Irwin, M. R. (2015). Mindfulness meditation and improvement in sleep quality and daytime impairment among older adults with sleep disturbances: a randomized clinical trial. *JAMA Internal Medicine*, *175*(4), 494. https://doi.org/10.1001/jamainternmed.2014.8081

Bonacaro, A. (2016). *Simulated mindfulness meditation: a major breakthrough in the management of chronic pain – Pain Nursing Magazine*. Pain Nursing Magazine. https://www.painnursing.it/simulated-mindfulness-meditation-a-major-breakthrough-in-the-management-of-chronic-pain/

Braganza, S., Young, J., Sweeny, A., & Brazil, V. (2018). oneED: Embedding a mindfulness-based wellness programme into an emergency department. *Emergency Medicine Australasia*, *30*(5), 678–686. https://doi.org/10.1111/1742-6723.12977

Brinkmann, A. E., Press, S. A., Helmert, E., Hautzinger, M., Khazan, I., & Vagedes, J. (2020). Comparing effectiveness of HRV-biofeedback and mindfulness for workplace stress reduction: A randomized controlled trial. *Applied Psychophysiology and Biofeedback*, 10.1007/s10484-020-09477-w. https://doi.org/10.1007/s10484-020-09477-w

Broderick, P. C., & Metz, S. (2009). *Learning to BREATHE: A pilot trial of a mindfulness curriculum for adolescents.* APA PsycNet. https://psycnet.apa.org/record/2011-06041-004

Brook, R. D., et al. (2013). Beyond medications and diet: alternative approaches to lowering blood pressure: a scientific statement from the American Heart Association. *Hypertension (Dallas, Tex. : 1979), 61*(6), 1360–1383. https://doi.org/10.1161/HYP.0b013e318293645f

Burg, J. M., Wolf, O. T., & Michalak, J. (2012). *Mindfulness as self-regulated attention: Associations with heart rate variability.* APA PsycNet. https://psycnet.apa.org/record/2012-16556-003

Büssing, A., et al. (2021). Awe/gratitude as an experiential aspect of spirituality and its association to perceived positive changes during the COVID-19 pandemic. *Frontiers in Psychiatry, 12*(10.3389/fpsyt.2021.642716). https://doi.org/10.3389/fpsyt.2021.642716

Caplan, J. (n.d.). *Aspects of sound healing: Toning, deep listening and freeing the natural voice.* Prema Yoga. https://www.premayogainstitute.com/pyi-blog/aspects-of-sound-healing-toning-deep-listening-and-freeing-the-natural-voice#:~:text=Toning%2C%20a%20practice%20involving%20the

Çay, M. (2017). The effect of cortisol level increasing due to stress in healthy young individuals on dynamic and static balance scores. *Northern Clinics of Istanbul, 5*(4). https://doi.org/10.14744/nci.2017.42103

Celestine, N. (2020, August 15). *What is mindful breathing? Exercises, scripts and videos.* PositivePsychology. https://positivepsychology.com/mindful-breathing/

Cherkin, D. C., et al. (2016). Effect of mindfulness-based stress reduction vs cognitive behavioral therapy or usual care on back pain and functional limitations in adults with chronic low back pain. *JAMA, 315*(12), 1240. https://doi.org/10.1001/jama.2016.2323

Cho, H., Ryu, S., Noh, J., & Lee, J. (2016). The effectiveness of daily mindful breathing practices on test anxiety of students. *PLOS ONE, 11*(10), e0164822. https://doi.org/10.1371/journal.pone.0164822

Conrad Stöppler, M. (2024, March 14). *Progressive muscle relaxation for stress and insomnia.* WebMD; WebMD. https://www.webmd.com/sleep-disorders/muscle-relaxation-for-stress-insomnia

Cop, I. (n.d.). *15 Quick easy ways to meditate: A beginner's guide to a lasting effective practice.* Insight Timer Blog. https://insighttimer.com/blog/meditation-techniques-for-beginners/

Creating a meditative environment in your home. (2018, November 13). Asana International Yoga Journal. https://asanajournal.com/creating-meditative-environment-home/#:~:text=To%20begin%20with%2C%20the%20physical

Creswell, J. D., et al. (2014). Brief mindfulness meditation training alters psychological and neuroendocrine responses to social evaluative stress. *Psychoneuroendocrinology, 44*(doi: 10.1016/j.psyneuen.2014.02.007. Epub 2014 Feb 23.), 1–12. https://doi.org/10.1016/j.psyneuen.2014.02.007

Creswell, J. D., Way, B. M., Eisenberger, N. I., & Lieberman, M. D. (2007). Neural correlates of dispositional mindfulness during affect labeling. *Psychosomatic Medicine, 69*(6), 560–565. https://doi.org/10.1097/psy.0b013e3180f6171f

DeMarco, C. (2022, February 8). *7 anxiety hacks: How to manage stress and worry in the moment.* MD Anderson Cancer Center. https://www.mdanderson.org/cancerwise/anxiety-hacks--7-tools-to-manage-stress-and-worry-in-the-moment.h00-159537378.html

Eagle, J. (2022, January 27). *The power of awe.* Live Conscious. https://liveconscious.com/2022/01/the-power-of-awe/

Elizabeth Scott. (2023, October 10). *How to reframe stressful situations.* Verywell Mind. https://www.verywellmind.com/cognitive-reframing-for-stress-management-3144872

Embedding mindfulness. (2020, February 28). You First Support Services. https://www.youfirstsupportservices.org.uk/blog/2020/02/28/embedding-mindfulness/27/

England, A. (2023, September 13). *How to stop catastrophizing and jumping to the worst-case scenario.* Verywell Mind. https://www.verywellmind.com/how-to-stop-catastrophizing-7693333

Enhance your meditation journey using a range of 280 varied techniques, spanning from tranquil breath monitoring to venturing into the astral realm. (2023, August 17). Scentopia. https://www.scentopia-singapore.com/280-best-meditation.html

Erisman, S. M., & Roemer, L. (2010). A preliminary investigation of the effects of experimentally induced mindfulness on emotional responding to film clips. *Emotion, 10*(1), 72–82. https://doi.org/10.1037/a0017162

Everyday mindfulness with Jon Kabat-Zinn. (n.d.). Mindful. https://www.mindful.org/everyday-mindfulness-with-jon-kabat-zinn/

Felver, J. C., Celis-de Hoyos, C. E., Tezanos, K., & Singh, N. N. (2016). *A systematic review of mindfulness-based interventions for youth in school settings.* APA PsycNet. https://psycnet.apa.org/record/2015-06589-001

Fredrickson, B. L., Cohn, M. A., Coffey, K. A., Pek, J., & Finkel, S. M. (2008). Open hearts build lives: Positive emotions, induced through loving-kindness meditation, build consequential personal resources. *Journal of Personality and Social Psychology, 95*(5), 1045–1062. https://doi.org/10.1037/a0013262

Getting started with mindful movement. (n.d.). Mindful. https://www.mindful.org/getting-started-with-mindful-movement/

Goldberg, S. B., Tucker, R. P., Greene, P. A., Davidson, R. J., Wampold, B. E., Kearney, D. J., & Simpson, T. L. (2018). Mindfulness-based interventions for psychiatric disorders: A systematic review and meta-analysis. *Clinical Psychology Review, 59*(59), 52–60. https://doi.org/10.1016/j.cpr.2017.10.011

Good, D. J., Lyddy, C. J., Glomb, T. M., Bono, J. E., Brown, K. W., Duffy, M. K., Baer, R. A., Brewer, J. A., & Lazar, S, S. W. (2016). *Contemplating mindfulness at work: An integrative review.* APA PsycNet. https://psycnet.apa.org/record/2015-55747-005

Grabowski, S. (n.d.). *23 Meditation techniques: A beginners guide to the many styles of practice.* THE MINDFUL STEWARD. https://themindfulsteward.com/mindfulness/23-meditation-techniques-a-beginners-guide-to-the-many-styles-of-practice/

Green, S. (n.d.). *101 Absolutely badass quotes about creativity.* Workflowmax. https://www.workflowmax.com/blog/101-absolutely-badass-quotes-about-creativity

Hafenbrack, A. C., Kinias, Z., & Barsade, S. G. (2013). Debiasing the mind through meditation. *Psychological Science*, *25*(2), 369–376. https://doi.org/10.1177/0956797613503853

Hafiz. (n.d.). *Personal growth quotes*. Www.goodreads.com. https://www.goodreads.com/quotes/tag/personal-growth

Haugmark, T., Hagen, K. B., Smedslund, G., & Zangi, H. A. (2019). Mindfulness- and acceptance-based interventions for patients with fibromyalgia – A systematic review and meta-analyses. *PLOS ONE*, *14*(9), e0221897. https://doi.org/10.1371/journal.pone.0221897

Holte, A. (2024). *Mindfulness and yoga: Complementary paths of health, healing, and wellbeing*. UC San Diego. https://cih.ucsd.edu/index.php/mbpti/blog/mindfulness-and-yoga-complementary-paths-health-healing-and-wellbeing

Hölzel, B. K., Carmody, J., Vangel, M., Congleton, C., Yerramsetti, S. M., Gard, T., & Lazar, S. W. (2011). Mindfulness practice leads to increases in regional brain gray matter density. *Psychiatry Research: Neuroimaging*, *191*(1), 36–43. https://doi.org/10.1016/j.pscychresns.2010.08.006

How (and why) to add morning meditation to your routine. (n.d.). Calm Blog. https://www.calm.com/blog/morning-meditation

How technology is transforming meditation. (n.d.). Vodafone Australia. https://www.vodafone.com.au/blog/lifestyle/how-technology-is-transforming-meditation

How to design your home using your senses. (n.d.). Moretti Interior Design . https://morettiinteriordesign.com/blog/psychology/how-to-design-your-home-using-your-senses/

How to meditate. (n.d.). Mindful. https://www.mindful.org/how-to-meditate/

Howard, A. (2022, April 19). *How does meditation affect your brain waves?* Psych Central. https://psychcentral.com/health/meditation-brain-waves

Hughes, J. W., Fresco, D. M., Myerscough, R., H. M. van Dulmen, M., Carlson, L. E., & Josephson, R. (2013). Randomized controlled trial of mindfulness-based stress reduction for prehypertension. *Psychosomatic Medicine, 75*(8), 721–728. https://doi.org/10.1097/psy.0b013e3182a3e4e5

Hülsheger, U. R., Alberts, H. J. E. M., Feinholdt, A., & Lang, J. W. B. (2013). Benefits of mindfulness at work: The role of mindfulness in emotion regulation, emotional exhaustion, and job satisfaction. *Journal of Applied Psychology, 98*(2), 310–325. https://doi.org/10.1037/a0031313

Indeed Editorial Team. (2024, April 8). *40 Quotes about time.* Https://Www.indeed.com/Career-Advice/Career-Development/Quotes-About-Time; Indeed.

Inner IDEA. (n.d.). *Meditation 101: Techniques, benefits, and a beginner's how-to.* Gaiam. https://www.gaiam.com/blogs/discover/meditation-101-techniques-benefits-and-a-beginner-s-how-to

Jacobs, T. L., Shaver, P. R., Epel, E. S., Zanesco, A. P., Aichele, S. R., Bridwell, D. A., Rosenberg, E. L., King, B. G., Maclean, K. A., Sahdra, B. K., Kemeny, M. E., Ferrer, E., Wallace, B. A., & Saron, C. D. (2013). Self-reported mindfulness and cortisol during a Shamatha meditation retreat. *Health Psychology: Official Journal of the Division of Health Psychology, American Psychological Association, 32*(10), 1104–1109. https://doi.org/10.1037/a0031362

Jain, S., Shapiro, S. L., Swanick, S., Roesch, S. C., Mills, P. J., Bell, I., & Schwartz, G. E. R. (2007). A randomized controlled trial of mindfulness meditation versus relaxation training: Effects on distress, positive states of mind, rumination, and distraction. *Annals of Behavioral Medicine*, *33*(1), 11–21. https://doi.org/10.1207/s15324796abm3301_2

Janssen, M., Heerkens, Y., Kuijer, W., van der Heijden, B., & Engels, J. (2018). Effects of mindfulness-based stress reduction on employees' mental health: A systematic review. *PLOS ONE*, *13*(1), e0191332. https://doi.org/10.1371/journal.pone.0191332

Jha, A. P., Stanley, E. A., Kiyonaga, A., Wong, L., & Gelfand, L. (2010). Examining the protective effects of mindfulness training on working memory capacity and affective experience. *Emotion*, *10*(1), 54–64. https://doi.org/10.1037/a0018438

June23. (2023, December 12). *7 Practical ways to incorporate mindfulness into daily tasks*. Medium. https://medium.com/@june23emile/7-practical-ways-to-incorporate-mindfulness-into-daily-tasks-395c2eb6a6b6

Kent, G. (n.d.). *Mindfulness quotes*. Goodreads. https://www.goodreads.com/quotes/tag/mindfulness

Keridan, K. (2020, October 30). *How to see things differently: Reframe to regain control*. Breathe Together Yoga. https://breathetogetheryoga.com/mindful/reframing/

Kim, J. G., Khil, T. G., Lim, Y., Park, K., Shin, M., & Shin, W. S. (2020). The psychological effects of a campus forest therapy program. *International Journal of Environmental Research and Public Health*, *17*(10), 3409. https://doi.org/10.3390/ijerph17103409

Kobayashi, H., Song, C., Ikei, H., Park, B.-J., Kagawa, T., & Miyazaki, Y. (2019). Combined effect of walking and forest environment on salivary cortisol concentration. *Frontiers in Public Health*, *7*(doi: 10.3389/fpubh.2019.00376). https://doi.org/10.3389/fpubh.2019.00376

Kozlowska, K., & Khan, R. (2011). A developmental, body-oriented intervention for children and adolescents with medically unexplained chronic pain. *Clinical Child Psychology and Psychiatry*, *16*(4), 575–598. https://doi.org/10.1177/1359104510387886

Kuyken, W., Byford, S., Taylor, R. S., Watkins, E., Holden, E., White, K., Barrett, B., Byng, R., Evans, A., Mullan, E., & Teasdale, J. D. (2008). Mindfulness-based cognitive therapy to prevent relapse in recurrent depression. *Journal of Consulting and Clinical Psychology*, *76*(6), 966–978. https://doi.org/10.1037/a0013786

La Torre, G., Raffone, A., Peruzzo, M., Calabrese, L., Cocchiara, R. A., D'Egidio, V., Leggieri, P. F., Dorelli, B., Zaffina, S., & Mannocci, A. (2020). Yoga and mindfulness as a tool for influencing affectivity, anxiety, mental health, and stress among healthcare workers: Results of a single-arm clinical trial. *Journal of Clinical Medicine*, *9*(4), 1037. https://doi.org/10.3390/jcm9041037

Lange, C. L. (2023, May 24). *50+ Thought-provoking quotes on technology*. Xoxoday. https://blog.xoxoday.com/events/famous-quotes-about-technology/

Lazar, S. W., Kerr, C. E., Wasserman, R. H., Gray, J. R., Greve, D. N., Treadway, M. T., McGarvey, M., Quinn, B. T., Dusek, J. A., Benson, H., Rauch, S. L., Moore, C. I., & Fischl, B. (2005). Meditation experience is associated with increased cortical thickness. *Neuroreport*, *16*(17), 1893–1897. https://www.ncbi.nlm.nih.gov/pmc/articles/PMC1361002/

Lit, R. (2023, March 13). *What happens when you meditate*. Stanford Magazine. https://stanfordmag.org/contents/what-happens-when-you-meditate

Liu, S., Liu, Y., & Ni, Y. (2018). A review of mindfulness improves decision making and future prospects. *Psychology*, *09*(02), 229–248. https://doi.org/10.4236/psych.2018.92015

Mackey, M. (n.d.). *Your environment can affect your meditation*. The Monroe Institute. https://www.monroeinstitute.org/blogs/blog/how-your-environment-can-affect-your-meditation

Majsiak, B., & Young, C. (2022, June 23). *7 Ways to practice breathwork for beginners*. Everyday Health. https://www.everydayhealth.com/alternative-health/living-with/ways-practice-breath-focused-meditation/

McInerney, L., & Morton-Aiken, J. (2024, April 2). *Embedded Meditation and mindfulness: An intentional turn in tutor training*. The Writing Center University of Wisconsin-Madison. https://dept.writing.wisc.edu/blog/embedded-meditation/

Meditation for beginners: An easy how-to guide for busy people. (n.d.). MEG D YOGA. https://www.megdyoga.com/blog/meditation-for-busy-people

Meditation myths and facts. (2021, May 15). Well Stated by Canyon Ranch. https://www.canyonranch.com/well-stated/post/meditation-myths-and-facts/

Meehan, J. (n.d.). *Mindfulness made simple for busy people*. Restorative Counseling. https://rcchicago.org/mindfulness-made-simple-for-busy-people/

Meister, A., Cheng, B. H., Dael, N., & Krings, F. (2022, July 5). *How to recover from work stress, according to science*. Harvard Business Review. https://hbr.org/2022/07/how-to-recover-from-work-stress-according-to-science

Mind Tools Content Team. (n.d.). *Mindful Listening*. MindTools. https://www.mindtools.com/af4nwki/mindful-listening

Mindful Staff. (n.d.). *How to start your day with meditation*. Mindful. https://www.mindful.org/how-to-start-your-day-with-meditation/

Mindfulness hacks: For budding entrepreneurs. (2023, July 20). AhaMastery. https://ahamastery.com/mindfulness-hacks-for-budding-entrepreneurs/

Mindtrick. (2023, November 17). *Daily serenity boost: Practical tips for embedding mindfulness in your lifestyle.* Medium. https://medium.com/@mindtrickstaff/daily-serenity-boost-practical-tips-for-embedding-mindfulness-in-your-lifestyle-17c9de4f6fad

Misra, S. N. (2023, January 15). *A busy person's guide to meditation & mindfulness.* Ananda. https://www.ananda.org/blog/a-busy-persons-guide-to-meditation-mindfulness/

Morbey, N. (2018, December 19). *Everything you need to know about meditation posture and structure.* Positively Mindful. https://www.positively-mindful.com/blog/everything-you-need-to-know-about-meditation-posture-and-structure

Morrison, A. B., Goolsarran, M., Rogers, S. L., & Jha, A. P. (2014). Taming a wandering attention: short-form mindfulness training in student cohorts. *Frontiers in Human Neuroscience, 7*(doi: 10.3389/fnhum.2013.00897). https://doi.org/10.3389/fnhum.2013.00897

Mrazek, M. D., Franklin, M. S., Phillips, D. T., Baird, B., & Schooler, J. W. (2013). Mindfulness training improves working memory capacity and GRE performance while reducing mind wandering. *Psychological Science, 24*(5), 776–781. https://doi.org/10.1177/0956797612459659

Mrazek, M. D., Smallwood, J., & Schooler, J. W. (2012). Mindfulness and mind-wandering: Finding convergence through opposing constructs. *Emotion, 12*(3), 442–448. https://doi.org/10.1037/a0026678

Nash, J. (2023, February 16). *Guided imagery in therapy: 20 Powerful scripts and techniques.* PositivePsychology. https://positivepsychology.com/guided-imagery-scripts/

National Center for Complementary and Integrative Health. (2022, June). *Meditation and mindfulness: What you need to know.* NCCIH. https://www.nccih.nih.gov/health/meditation-and-mindfulness-what-you-need-to-know

Nelson, E. (2024, April 10). *Meditation myths busted: Discover the truth about Zen, mindfulness, and more!* Medium. https://medium.com/@deliberateelsa/meditation-myths-busted-discover-the-truth-about-zen-mindfulness-and-more-54423081c532

Nguyen, T. (2020, April 8). *4 Tools in the new (digital) age of meditation.* NUVO. https://nuvomagazine.com/business/the-new-digital-age-of-meditation

Nyklíček, I., & Kuijpers, K. F. (2008). Effects of mindfulness-based stress reduction intervention on psychological well-being and quality of life: is increased mindfulness indeed the mechanism? *Annals of Behavioral Medicine, 35*(3), 331–340. https://doi.org/10.1007/s12160-008-9030-2

O'Brien, E. (2021, August 18). *What is mindfulness, really?* Yoga Journal. https://www.yogajournal.com/lifestyle/what-is-mindfulness/

Ophir, E., Nass, C., & Wagner, A. D. (2009). Cognitive control in media multitaskers. *Proceedings of the National Academy of Sciences, 106*(37), 15583–15587. https://doi.org/10.1073/pnas.0903620106

Ostafin, B. D., & Kassman, K. T. (2012). Stepping out of history: Mindfulness improves insight problem solving. *Consciousness and Cognition, 21*(2), 1031–1036. https://doi.org/10.1016/j.concog.2012.02.014

Paredes, P. E., Hamdan, N. A.-H., Clark, D., Cai, C., Ju, W., & Landay, J. A. (2017). Evaluating in-car movements in the design of mindful commute interventions: Exploratory study. *Journal of Medical Internet Research*, *19*(12). https://doi.org/10.2196/jmir.6983

Perls, F. (n.d.). *Senses quote*. Goodreads. https://www.goodreads.com/quotes/tag/senses

Plews-Ogan, M., Owens, J. E., Goodman, M., Wolfe, P., & Schorling, J. (2005). Brief report: A pilot study evaluating mindfulness-based stress reduction and massage for the management of chronic pain. *Journal of General Internal Medicine*, *20*(12), 1136–1138. https://doi.org/10.1111/j.1525-1497.2005.0247.x

Psy.D, R. D. S. (2015, October 6). *A mindful worker is a happier worker*. Harvard Health. https://www.health.harvard.edu/blog/a-mindful-worker-is-a-happier-worker-201510068391

Raupp, A. (2014, August 20). *Why are we all so busy?* HuffPost. https://www.huffpost.com/entry/why-are-we-all-so-busy_b_5691128

Ray, A. (n.d.). *Meditation quotes*. Goodreads. https://www.goodreads.com/quotes/tag/meditation

Raypole, C. (2024, January 29). *30 Grounding techniques to quiet distressing thoughts*. Healthline. https://www.healthline.com/health/grounding-techniques

Reitz, M., & Chaskalson, M. (2020, August 19). *Why your team should practice collective mindfulness*. Harvard Business Review. https://hbr.org/2020/08/why-your-team-should-practice-collective-mindfulness

Rekhi, S. (n.d.). *Meditation techniques: Definitions, examples & tips*. The Berkeley Well-Being Institute.

https://www.berkeleywellbeing.com/meditation-techniques.html

Resnick, A. (2021, July 12). *Meditation facts: Why you don't have to clear your mind.* Verywell Mind. https://www.verywellmind.com/meditation-myths-why-clearing-your-mind-is-a-myth-5179587

Riopel, L. (2019a, September 25). *30 Meditation exercises and activities to practice today.* PositivePsychology. https://positivepsychology.com/meditation-exercises-activities/#:~:text=One%20quick%20and%20fun%20mindfulness

Riopel, L. (2019b, November 28). *28 Best meditation techniques for beginners to learn.* PositivePsychology. https://positivepsychology.com/meditation-techniques-beginners/

Rodriguez, M. (2021, April 23). *Myths vs. the truth about mindfulness meditation, with Marta Brzosko.* Medium. https://betterhumans.pub/myths-vs-the-truth-about-mindfulness-meditation-with-marta-brzosko-43a0fb2b6c5a

Ruedy, N. E., & Schweitze, M. E. (2010). *In the moment: The effect of mindfulness on ethical decision making.* APA PsycNet. https://psycnet.apa.org/record/2011-11513-007

Ruedy, N., & Schweitzer, M. E. (2010, September). *In the moment: The effect of mindfulness on ethical decision making.* ResearchGate. https://www.researchgate.net/publication/225332974_In_the_Moment_The_Effect_of_Mindfulness_on_Ethical_Decision_Making

Safi, O. (2014, November 6). *The disease of being busy.* The on Being Project. https://onbeing.org/blog/the-disease-of-being-busy/

Sauber Millacci, T. (2017, June 18). *49 Profound mindfulness quotes to inspire your practice.* PositivePsychology. https://positivepsychology.com/mindfulness-quotes/#mindfulness-quotes

Sauer, S., & Baer, R. A. (2010). *Mindfulness and decentering as mechanisms of change in mindfulness- and acceptance-based interventions.* APA PsycNet. https://psycnet.apa.org/record/2010-08791-001

Schofield, T. P., Creswell, J. D., & Denson, T. F. (2015). Brief mindfulness induction reduces inattentional blindness. *Consciousness and Cognition, 37*(https://doi.org/10.1016/j.concog.2015.08.007), 63–70. https://doi.org/10.1016/j.concog.2015.08.007

Scott, E. (2022, April 20). *The benefits of meditation for stress management.* Verywell Mind; Verywell Mind. https://www.verywellmind.com/meditation-4157199

Scott, E. (2024a, January 22). *Focused meditation: How to start a practice.* Verywell Mind. https://www.verywellmind.com/practice-focused-meditation-3144785

Scott, E. (2024b, February 12). *What is body scan meditation?* Verywell Mind. https://www.verywellmind.com/body-scan-meditation-why-and-how-3144782

Segalas, X. (2023, September 21). *Six essential tips for designing your sacred meditation space for success.* Medium. https://medium.com/@segalascreatives/6-essential-tips-for-designing-your-sacred-meditation-space-for-success-78ea28d7bbd6

Selig, M. (2017, March 1). *12 Quick mini-meditations to calm your mind and body.* Psychology Today. https://www.psychologytoday.com/us/blog/changepower/201703/12-quick-mini-meditations-calm-your-mind-and-body

Sensory decoration: the trend that will sharpen the senses. (2022, September 29). L'Officiel. https://www.lofficielibiza.com/design/sensory-decoration-the-trend-that-will-sharpen-the-senses

Shabb, H. (2018, September 24). *The importance of creating space for yourself*. The Stanford Daily. https://stanforddaily.com/2018/09/24/the-importance-of-creating-space-for-yourself/

Shah, P. (2024, January 13). *Meditation space: The language of silence*. The Architects Diary. https://thearchitectsdiary.com/meditation-space-the-language-of-silence/

Shah, S., & Ullman, S. (2022, June 17). *20 Must-know meditation tips and techniques for beginners*. Business Insider. https://www.businessinsider.com/guides/health/mental-health/meditation-tips-for-beginners

Sherrell, Z. (2022, October 27). *What are the physical and mental benefits of meditation?* Medical News Today. https://www.medicalnewstoday.com/articles/benefits-of-meditation

Shonin, E., Van Gordon, W., Dunn, T. J., Singh, N. N., & Griffiths, M. D. (2014). *Meditation Awareness Training (MAT) for work-related wellbeing and job performance: A randomised controlled trial*. APA PsycNet. https://psycnet.apa.org/record/2014-33050-001

Shukla, S. (n.d.). *Knowing your worth quotes*. Goodreads. https://www.goodreads.com/quotes/tag/knowing-your-worth

Singh, P. (2024, May 6). *Top meditation app statistics to know in 2022*. Appinventiv. https://appinventiv.com/blog/latest-meditation-app-statistics/

Singh, Y., Sharma, R., & Talwar, A. (2012). Immediate and long-term effects of meditation on acute stress reactivity, cognitive functions, and intelligence. *Alternative Therapies in Health and Medicine*, *18*(6), 46–53. https://pubmed.ncbi.nlm.nih.gov/23251943/

Sivananda, S. (n.d.). *Experiences and obstacles during meditation*. The Divine Life Society. https://www.sivanandaonline.org/?cmd=displaysection§ion_id=936

Sloww. (2018, September 25). *Busyness 101: Why are we so busy in modern life? (7 hypotheses)*. Medium. https://medium.com/@slowwco/busyness-101-why-are-we-so-busy-in-modern-life-7-hypotheses-6f896826ee37

Spurgeon, C. H. (2010). *Anxiety quotes*. Goodreads. https://www.goodreads.com/quotes/tag/anxiety

Stress. (2023, February 21). World Health Organization. https://www.who.int//news-room/questions-and-answers/item/stress/?gad_source=1&gclid=Cj0KCQjwmMayBhDuARIsAM9HM8frV_87MoDRVzADKJglQExCTQCToFbWHF5J7SvpkDMetP74tV3h8e0aAmflEALw_wcB

Stress effects on the body. (2023, March 8). American Psychological Association; American Psychological Association. https://www.apa.org/topics/stress/body

Stulberg, B. (2017, December 9). *The 5 pillars of holistic peak performance*. Medium. https://medium.com/personal-growth/the-5-pillars-of-holistic-peak-performance-8a5b59b8f338

Subrameyer, R. (2019, December 13). *Accelerating your value through productivity, mindfulness and social hacks*. Medium. https://medium.com/@epsilon11/accelerating-your-value-through-productivity-mindfulness-and-social-hacks-35ad41ccc37a

Sugiura, T., & Sugiura, Y. (2014). Common factors of meditation, focusing, and cognitive behavioral therapy: Longitudinal relation of self-report measures to worry, depressive, and obsessive-compulsive symptoms among nonclinical students. *Mindfulness, 6*(3), 610–623. https://doi.org/10.1007/s12671-014-0296-0

Sutton, J. (2019, June 19). *20+ Health benefits of meditation according to science.* PositivePsychology. https://positivepsychology.com/benefits-of-meditation/

Sutton, J. (2021, September 30). *Workplace stress management: 11 Best strategies & worksheets.* PositivePsychology. https://positivepsychology.com/workplace-stress-management/

Sweet, J. (2020, May 30). *11 Meditation myths you should stop believing.* Forbes. https://www.forbes.com/sites/jonisweet/2020/05/30/11-meditation-myths-you-should-stop-believing/?sh=4a91c02d55b6

Tang, Y.-Y. ., Ma, Y., Wang, J., Fan, Y., Feng, S., Lu, Q., Yu, Q., Sui, D., Rothbart, M. K., Fan, M., & Posner, M. I. (2007). Short-term meditation training improves attention and self-regulation. *Proceedings of the National Academy of Sciences, 104*(43), 17152–17156. https://doi.org/10.1073/pnas.0707678104

Tarrant, J. (2023, April 7). *Technology-assisted meditation.* Psychology Today. https://www.psychologytoday.com/us/blog/choosing-your-meditation-style/202304/technology-assisted-meditation

Teasdale, J. D., Segal, Z. V., J. Mark G. Williams, Ridgeway, V. A., Soulsby, J. M., & Lau, M. A. (2000). Prevention of relapse/recurrence in major depression by mindfulness-based cognitive therapy. *Journal of Consulting and Clinical Psychology, 68*(4), 615–623. https://doi.org/10.1037//0022-006x.68.4.615

Technology-assisted meditation: Definition and benefits. (n.d.). SOLUM ESL. https://www.solum-group.com/technology-assisted-meditation-definition-and-benefits

Tee-Melegrito, R. A. (2023, May 5). *Cortisol and stress: What is the connection?* Medical News Today. https://www.medicalnewstoday.com/articles/cortisol-and-stress

10 Simple ways to integrate mindfulness into your daily routine. (n.d.). Search inside Yourself. https://siyli.org/10-simple-ways-to-integrate-mindfulness-into-your-daily-routine/

Thau, L., Gandhi, J., & Sharma, S. (2023, August 28). *Physiology, cortisol.* National Library of Medicine; StatPearls Publishing. https://www.ncbi.nlm.nih.gov/books/NBK538239/

The 5 pillars of resilience. (2022, June 15). The Wellbeing Project. https://thewellbeingproject.co.uk/insight/the-5-pillars-of-resilience/

The best meditation apps. (2023, November 15). *The New York Times.* https://www.nytimes.com/wirecutter/reviews/best-meditation-apps/

The Editors at Chopra.com. (2013, February 22). *7 Myths of meditation.* Chopra. https://chopra.com/blogs/meditation/7-myths-of-meditation

The Psychology of home decor: How Your surroundings can impact your mood. (n.d.). Virginia Home & Lifestyle. https://www.virginiahomeandlifestyle.com/blog-home/gmk2uv5dkzqoju8p9o0jkel0d2q5h0

Think Interior. (2023, May 5). *Recognizing the significance of space and its purpose.* Medium.

https://academythinkinteriordesign.medium.com/recognizing-the-significance-of-space-and-its-purpose-7ef76691edae

Thinkrightme. (2022, October 13). *What are the short term and long term benefits of meditation?* Medium. https://medium.com/@think-right-me/what-are-the-short-term-and-long-term-benefits-of-meditation-9424cb047d12

33 Of the best meditation quotes. (n.d.). Headspace. https://www.headspace.com/meditation/quotes

Tjaša Kermavnar, & Desmet, A. (2024). Technology and meditation: Exploring the challenges and benefits of a physical device to support meditation routine. *Multimodal Technologies and Interaction*, *8*(2), 9–9. https://doi.org/10.3390/mti8020009

Trungpa, C. (2022, August 16). *105 Mindfulness quotes for employee health and wellness.* Vantage Fit. https://www.vantagefit.io/blog/mindfulness-quotes/

Tugade, M. M., Fredrickson, B. L., & Feldman Barrett, L. (2004). Psychological resilience and positive emotional granularity: Examining the benefits of positive emotions on coping and health. *Journal of Personality*, *72*(6), 1161–1190. https://doi.org/10.1111/j.1467-6494.2004.00294.x

12 Science-based benefits of meditation. (2022, January 31). Humanitas University. https://www.hunimed.eu/news/12-science-based-benefits-of-meditation/#:~:text=Another%20study%20of%201%2C300%20people

25 Quick ways to reduce stress. (n.d.). Colorado Law. https://www.colorado.edu/law/25-quick-ways-reduce-stress

University of Kentucky, & Maharishi University. (2007, December 5). *Transcendental meditation effective in reducing high blood pressure, Study*

Shows. ScienceDaily. https://www.sciencedaily.com/releases/2007/12/071204121953.htm

Ussher, M., Spatz, A., Copland, C., Nicolaou, A., Cargill, A., Amini-Tabrizi, N., & McCracken, L. M. (2012). Immediate effects of a brief mindfulness-based body scan on patients with chronic pain. *Journal of Behavioral Medicine, 37*(1), 127–134. https://doi.org/10.1007/s10865-012-9466-5

Utopian Fold. (2023, January 10). *Mindfulness at home: How to transform your space into a sanctuary of peace*. Ongrid Design. https://ongrid.design/blogs/trending-designs/mindfulness-at-home-how-to-transform-your-space-into-a-sanctuary-of-peace

Vo, K. (2024, March 29). *100 Mindfulness quotes to go from stress to blessed at work*. Flexos. https://www.flexos.work/tools/mindfulness-quotes-for-work

Vujanovic, A. A., Niles, B., Pietrefesa, A., Schmertz, S. K., & Potter, C. M. (2013). *Mindfulness in the treatment of posttraumatic stress disorder among military veterans*. APA PsycNet. https://psycnet.apa.org/record/2013-25345-003

WebMD Editorial Contributors. (2024, February 20). *What to know about work burnout*. WebMD. https://www.webmd.com/mental-health/what-to-know-about-work-burnout

Weinstein, N., Brown, K. W., & Ryan, R. M. (2009). *A multi-method examination of the effects of mindfulness on stress attribution, coping, and emotional well-being*. APA PsycNet. https://psycnet.apa.org/record/2009-06400-009

Wenneberg, S. R., Schneider, R. H., Walton, K. G., Maclean, C. R., Levitsky, D. K., Salerno, J. W., Wallace, R. K., Mandarino, J. V., Rainforth, M. V., & Waziri, R. (1997). A controlled study of the effects of the transcendental meditation program on cardiovascular reactivity and ambulatory blood pressure. *The International Journal of Neuroscience, 89*(1-2), 15–28. https://doi.org/10.3109/00207459708988461

West, J., Otte, C., Geher, K., Johnson, J., & Mohr, D. C. (2004). Effects of hatha yoga and African dance on perceived stress, affect, and salivary cortisol. *Annals of Behavioral Medicine, 28*(2), 114–118. https://doi.org/10.1207/s15324796abm2802_6

West, M. (2022, April 21). *What to know about guided imagery.* Medical News Today. https://www.medicalnewstoday.com/articles/guided-imagery

What are the benefits of vocal toning? (n.d.). Ruth Ratliff. https://www.ruthratliff.com/blog/what-are-the-benefits-of-vocal-toning

What is a sound bath meditation & how can it benefit you? (n.d.). Calm Blog. https://www.calm.com/blog/sound-bath

What is bilateral stimulation? (n.d.). Anxiety Release. https://anxietyreleaseapp.com/what-is-bilateral-stimulation/

What to focus on during meditation: 20 Ideas. (n.d.). Search Inside Yourself. https://siyli.org/meditation-20-ideas/

Will Knight. (2005, April 22). *"Info-mania" dents IQ more than marijuana.* New Scientist. https://www.newscientist.com/article/dn7298-info-mania-dents-iq-more-than-marijuana/

Williamson, E., & Gaston, N. (2020, August 5). Nature and nurture: Connecting conservation and wellbeing. *National Library Wellington.* https://natlib.govt.nz/blog/posts/nature-and-nurture-connecting-conservation-and-wellbeing

Wisner, W. (2023, July 17). *How a brain dump can help you relieve stress.* Verywell Mind. https://www.verywellmind.com/what-is-a-brain-dump-7111793

Woodyard, C. (2011). Exploring the therapeutic effects of yoga and its ability to increase quality of life. *International Journal of Yoga, 4*(2), 49–54. https://doi.org/10.4103/0973-6131.85485

Workplace burnout: Causes, effects, and solutions. (2019, June 6). Western Governors University; Western Governors University. https://www.wgu.edu/blog/workplace-burnout-causes-effects-solutions1906.html

Yang, C.-H., Hakun, J. G., Roque, N., Sliwinski, M. J., & Conroy, D. E. (2021). Mindful walking and cognition in older adults: A proof of concept study using in-lab and ambulatory cognitive measures. *Preventive Medicine Reports, 23*(10.1016/j.pmedr.2021.101490), 101490. https://doi.org/10.1016/j.pmedr.2021.101490

Your Headspace Mindfulness & Meditation Experts. (n.d.). *Types of meditation.* Headspace. https://www.headspace.com/meditation/techniques

Yukawa, J. (n.d.). *6 Mindful hacks to boost productivity, energy, and reduce stress.* Oxford Leadership. https://www.oxfordleadership.com/5-mindful-hacks-to-boost-your-productivity-and-reduce-stress/

Zanesco, A. P., Denkova, E., & Jha, A. P. (2024). *Mind-wandering increases in frequency over time during task performance: An individual-participant meta-analytic review.* APA PsycNet. https://psycnet.apa.org/fulltext/2024-58385-001.html

Zeidan, F., Emerson, N. M., Farris, S. R., Ray, J. N., Jung, Y., McHaffie, J. G., & Coghill, R. C. (2015). Mindfulness meditation-based pain relief employs different neural mechanisms than placebo and sham mindfulness meditation-induced analgesia. *Journal of Neuroscience, 35*(46), 15307–15325. https://doi.org/10.1523/jneurosci.2542-15.2015

Zeidan, F., Johnson, S. K., Diamond, B. J., David, Z., & Goolkasian, P. (2010). Mindfulness meditation improves cognition: Evidence of brief mental training. *Consciousness and Cognition*, *19*(2), 597–605. https://doi.org/10.1016/j.concog.2010.03.014

Zeidan, F., Martucci, K. T., Kraft, R. A., Gordon, N. S., McHaffie, J. G., & Coghill, R. C. (2011). Brain mechanisms supporting the modulation of pain by mindfulness meditation. *Journal of Neuroscience*, *31*(14), 5540–5548. https://doi.org/10.1523/jneurosci.5791-10.2011

Made in the USA
Columbia, SC
18 January 2025